# BEHIND SOVIET LINES

## Hitler's Brandenburgers capture
## the Maikop Oilfields 1942

# DAVID R. HIGGINS

First published in Great Britain in 2014 by Osprey Publishing,
PO Box 883, Oxford, OX1 9PL, UK
PO Box 3985, New York, NY 10185-3985, USA
E-mail: info@ospreypublishing.com

Osprey Publishing is part of the Osprey Group

A CIP catalogue record for this book is available from the British Library

Print ISBN: 978 1 78200 599 5
PDF ebook ISBN: 978 1 78200 600 8
ePub ebook ISBN: 978 1 78200 601 5

Index by Alan Thatcher
Typeset in Sabon
Maps by bounford.com
3D BEV by Alan Gilliland
Originated by PDQ Media, Bungay, UK
Printed in China through Worldprint Ltd

14 15 16 17 18 10 9 8 7 6 5 4 3 2 1

Osprey Publishing is supporting the Woodland Trust, the UK's leading
woodland conservation charity, by funding the dedication of trees.

www.ospreypublishing.co.uk

## ACKNOWLEDGEMENTS

I would like to thank the following individuals for their kind support,
without which this book and my other military history endeavours might
not have been possible: Joseph Miranda, editor in chief, *Strategy & Tactics*
magazine; Colonel (ret.) Jerry D. Morelock, PhD, editor in chief, *Armchair
General* magazine; Michael Heinz; Vadim Anokhin; Lyubov Glazkova;
Vladimir Volkov; Youriy Mishurin; Helen Di; Sergey Zherdev; and my editors
Nick Reynolds and Tom Milner. Any errors or omissions in this work were
certainly unintended, and I alone bear responsibility for them.

## COVER ART

On 10 August 1942, as the German SS Division (Motorized) Wiking
approached Belorechensk, truck-borne Brandenburger special forces
secured the bridge over the Belaya River to aid the division's thrust toward
Tuapse. Dressed in Red Army uniforms, riding in captured Soviet trucks and
armed with PPSh-41 machine pistols, the Brandenburgers crossed the
bridge, shot the crew of a nearby tanker truck, then quickly cut the main
detonation wire and remove the explosives from the bridge piers.

## ARTISTS' NOTE

Readers may care to note that the original paintings from which the
colour plates of this book were prepared are available for private sale.
All reproduction copyright whatsoever is retained by the Publishers.
The Publishers regret that they can enter into no correspondence upon
this matter.

Enquiries regarding the battlescene and figure paintings should be
addressed to Johnny Shumate (shumate1977@gmail.com), and enquiries
regarding the cover painting to Mark Stacey (mark@mrstacey.plus.com).

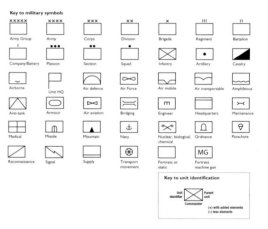

# COMPARATIVE COMMISSIONED RANKS

| British Army | Heer | Waffen-SS | Soviet |
|---|---|---|---|
| n/a | Reichsmarschall | n/a | Marshal |
| n/a | n/a | Reichsführer-SS | n/a |
| Field marshal | Generalfeldmarschall | n/a | General of the Army |
| General | Generaloberst | SS-Oberstgruppenführer | Colonel-General |
| Lieutenant-general | General der Infanterie | SS-Obergruppenführer | Lieutenant-General |
| Major-general | Generalleutnant | SS-Gruppenführer | Major-General |
| Brigadier | Generalmajor | SS-Brigadeführer | n/a |
| n/a | n/a | SS-Oberführer | n/a |
| Colonel | Oberst | SS-Standartenführer | Colonel |
| Lieutenant-colonel | Oberstleutnant | SS-Obersturmbannführer | Lieutenant-Colonel |
| Major | Major | SS-Sturmbannführer | Major |
| Captain | Hauptmann/Rittmeister | SS-Hauptsturmführer | Captain |
| Lieutenant | Oberleutnant | SS-Obersturmführer | Lieutenant |
| 2nd lieutenant | Leutnant | SS-Untersturmführer | Lieutenant |

# CONTENTS

# INTRODUCTION

For more than a year after the start of World War II in Europe, the German Army and Luftwaffe achieved a string of decisive victories against Poland, the Low Countries, Denmark, Norway, and most importantly against France – its historic rival, and promoter of the punitive Versailles Treaty that was intended to cripple Germany's economy and military following the Great War. Propaganda credited German use of modern, all-arms armoured, mechanized, and aerial forces, something with which the vanquished were eager to concur, in part to deflect blame from their own deficiencies in leadership, doctrine, and foresight. As these campaigns were of relatively limited space and duration, problems related to logistics, casualty replacement, and an overwhelmingly foot and horse-bound army did not unduly hinder the Wehrmacht maintaining a rapid battlefield tempo. With such accomplishments won at significantly less cost than during the previous world war, by early 1941 Germany's Führer and Reichskanzler, Adolf Hitler, felt confident to enact his long-desired plan to defeat Communist Russia, create *Lebensraum* ('living space') for colonization, and control Eastern Europe's labour potential, foodstuffs, and raw materials. Although as part of their recently signed Treaty of Non-Aggression and subsequent Commercial Agreement, the Soviets had been providing their new ally with considerable amounts of such items, including grain, iron ore, and oil, in exchange for military technologies and manufacturing capabilities, Hitler remained firm in his conviction to eliminate his political and ideological foe in what was expected to be another short campaign not exceeding six weeks.

Throughout the 1930s, Germany seemed impossibly far from producing enough food and especially fuel to weather a potentially long war, as roughly two-thirds of its fuel was imported from North and South America. Although Hitler pushed for domestic production of a synthetic alternative to offset potential wartime blockade shortages, the effort lacked effective leadership and coordination until 1938, when Luftwaffe Commander-in-Chief, Hermann Göring, was placed in charge of the existing 'Four Year Plan', in

which various experts worked to move the nation toward economic independence and a wartime mobilization. Although the group steadily achieved most of its goals, including increasing domestic oil production, any incentive to implement an effective, realistic fuel policy was hindered by the accumulation of conquered assets. Just one year into the war, the nation's petroleum resources had increased by more than half via the acquisition of the oil refineries and storage facilities at Pechelbronn (Alsace), La Rochelle (France), Rotterdam (Netherlands), Antwerp (Belgium), Austria, and elsewhere. As the defeated Polish and Western forces had largely refrained from destroying or damaging their oil production facilities, German leaders hoped that such a scenario would hold true with the Soviets, and beyond that, the oil-rich Middle East.

However significant Germany's recent petroleum conquests were, they paled in comparison to what resulted from its influence over Rumania, the world's fourth largest oil producer in 1936. Having recently pressured the nation into a bilateral economic agreement, Germany had considerable control over its ally's resources, including the Ploesti petroleum facilities, which contributed roughly one-third of its needs and over 95 per cent of crude oil imports, and remained its most important foreign supplier until the summer of 1944. Although the Reich's fuel production assets and reserves had increased considerably, these fields were becoming exhausted, and they could ill afford expending the necessary money and effort required to explore, drill, and exploit new options.

As Europe's largest oil production and refining facility, Ploesti (Rumania) provided the majority of Germany's imported oil by early 1941. Estimates that domestic and occupied reserves would be exhausted by August, however, prompted Germany to focus on securing the oil-producing Caucasus region to make up the difference. (NARA)

As early as 31 July 1940, Hitler revealed to senior commanders his intention to shatter Russia 'to its roots with one blow', after which the German Army would secure the Caucasus and the primary Soviet oil-producing area around Baku, one of the world's most productive fields, and others, including Grozny, Krasnodar, and Maikop. With western continental Europe secure for the foreseeable future, and the threat of a two-front war seemingly averted, Hitler unleashed Operation *Barbarossa* on 22 June 1941. With the Wehrmacht now fielding over three million men in the east, and thousands of motorized vehicles and aircraft, the need to secure these assets for the greatly expanding war effort was considered paramount. Within a few weeks, Germany had succeeded in overrunning a considerable amount of territory, and destroying or capturing large numbers of men and quantities of materiel – something that would have been impossible had they not received the more than half a billion Reichsmarks (US \$3.3bn today) in commercial goods shipments from its former ally over the preceding year.

The early estimate for victory in the east was increasingly unrealistic, however, as their reeling adversary remained in the field despite the cost. ByDecember ever-lengthening logistics, poor weather and terrain, and an influx of Soviet reinforcements from other sectors, once it became known that Japan was directing its attention toward the Pacific rather than Russia and would not be an immediate threat, meant that the Germans were forced to adopt a defensive stance along the 1,800km front from Leningrad to Rostov-on-Don. In addition to maintaining a presence in captured territories, resources were further stretched by a campaign in North Africa to support Italy's floundering effort against the British, and Finland's Continuation War against their common Soviet enemy. Having thus suffered its first significant battlefield setback of the war, and faced with the prospect of a lengthy conflict, Hitler worried that his armed forces would soon grind to a halt for want of resources, particularly petroleum, oil, and lubricants.

During the winter of 1941–42, economic considerations were a factor in the formulation of a new strategy, as was the poor state of German forces in the east. Having unwisely declared war against the United States in support of Japan, Hitler feared a Soviet air campaign against the oilfields around Ploesti and domestic synthetic production launched from airfields in the Crimean Peninsula, which had yet to be subdued. By continuing eastward and capturing the Caucasus, the greater distances would negate this threat, likely eliminate Stalin's ability to continue the war, and open a route to the Middle East. Should German efforts succeed, they would deliver a powerful blow to the Soviet economy and war effort, and enable the waging of a prolonged war against an increasing number of Allied nations.

# ORIGINS

## Germany's special forces

At the turn of the 20th century, the increasing likelihood of a war in Europe had promoted a massive armed forces expansion, which commensurately required greater national production output, transportation infrastructure, and organization to maintain effective command and control and to support forces in the field for a prolonged period of attritional fighting. Once committed to combat operations, in World War I, these predominantly conscripted armies occupied fronts of several hundred kilometres. With a Western Front considerably shorter than in the east, what had started as a war of relative movement soon degenerated into a continuous line of in-depth, reinforced defensive positions, which all but eliminated open flanks that could be turned, penetrated, and exploited. Lacking the combined numbers and resources of their British, French, and Russian adversaries, by mid-war, German infantry increasingly adopted infiltration tactics developed in the more fluid east and applied them in the west as a means of breaking the operational deadlock. Although these specially trained assault infantry proved effective in many offensives between 1916 and 1918, being overwhelmingly foot-bound they lacked the endurance to fully exploit battlefield gains.

### Lettow-Vorbeck's colonial warfare

In contrast to such battles, the secondary conflict zones of World War I, such as in colonial Africa, promoted a guerrilla campaign, in which much smaller formations used manoeuvre, subterfuge, reconnaissance, and infiltration to achieve success or avoid defeat. In defence of Imperial Germany's East African colony, Oberstleutnant Paul Emil von Lettow-Vorbeck worked to achieve a decisive victory against British forces and to siphon as much of their men and materiel from the primary Western Front theatre as possible. Extensively trained and having served on the Prussian (German) General Staff, he had ascended to his position based on merit, and not due to his noble ancestry. Outnumbered, he initially applied his considerable combat experience gained in China and German South-West Africa to fight a campaign based on a conventional war of movement, in which he believed his command could defeat or evade a more numerous opponent via bold enveloping attacks. To fight such a campaign, he utilized German officers and locally recruited Askaris, a professional–native mix that other colonial powers incorporated with varying degrees of success to avoid the cost and effort of maintaining a large, more established presence. Having transitioned these so-called 'Schütztruppe' from conducting counter-insurgency and guerrilla raids against minor economic targets to a conventional war of movement, Lettow-Vorbeck achieved considerable success.

Lettow-Vorbeck's seemingly isolated command conducted a series of effective actions that outmanoeuvred the British forces sent against him. In November, he bested an amphibious landing at the port of Tanga, and although outnumbered 8:1, captured considerable amounts of weapons and supplies to maintain his forces in the field. Unlike his adversary, Lettow-Vorbeck coordinated closely with his Askaris, and equipped them with modern weapons, artillery, uniforms when available, as well as training them. Such trust and interaction paid battlefield dividends, as he used movement to repeatedly evade superior numbers or strike for vulnerable subsets. If presented with an opportunity, he was always eager to attack using tactics that exploited the region's rugged environment, and had an ability to perceive the repercussions of battlefield action several steps ahead. Although his strength lay in detailed training and discipline, his units excelled because of his insistence on excellence and perfection in all endeavours, especially road marching, drill, and marksmanship. He made excellent use of weather conditions, and even incorporated the surrounding wildlife, as evidenced by his ordering machine-gun crews to target hives of African killer bees along a British march route.

In October, the German forces defeated the larger British force at Mahiwa, while suffering just one-sixteenth of their casualties. Ultimately, the Allies captured territory, but failed to completely defeat Lettow-Vorbeck, who due to declining numbers withdrew south and moved to guerrilla warfare to compensate. Cut off from their supply lines, his forces lived off the land and used captured stores, weapons, and ammunition to remain viable. Throughout the war, Lettow-Vorbeck inflicted a disproportionate number of casualties, but dwindling supplies and being outnumbered, especially with additional enemy forces from the Belgian Congo, steadily took a toll. Forced to abandon the colony and withdraw into Mozambique, and finally Northern Rhodesia, he agreed a ceasefire three days after the war-ending armistice. Although he made a good conventional field commander, his lack of inter-personal skills, arrogance, and intractability had distanced Lettow-Vorbeck from his subordinates and superiors alike. His determination, however, resulted in his Schütztruppe being celebrated in Germany as the only army not to have been defeated. But over the next two decades, the doctrine and application of special operations formations was largely ignored as most nations continued to favour large, conventional armed forces at the virtual exclusion of unorthodox options.

# World War II and the Brandenburgers

When war returned to Europe, however, the potential of special units was re-examined. During the Polish campaign in September 1939, OKW (Oberkommando der Wehrmacht, or Armed Forces High Command), experimented with a formation of Polish-speaking *Volksdeutsche* (ethnic Germans living abroad) called Bataillon Ebbinghaus that conducted irregular missions such as infiltration, sabotage, securing roads, bridges, and similar assets, and generally facilitating German progress and sowing confusion within enemy ranks, especially during the initial border actions. At the month-long fight's conclusion, however, their unorthodox methods, heavy casualties, and incidents of killing civilians proved too much for the Prussian High Command, which disbanded the unit as unsoldierly and too radical.

Having headed the Abwehr since 1 January 1935, Wilhelm Canaris' success in expanding the intelligence agency's scope and effectiveness earned him a promotion to admiral on 1 January 1941. (Archiv M. Heinz)

However, seeing a continued use for such 'special soldiers', albeit in a more professional iteration, Vizeadmiral (Vice Admiral) Wilhelm Canaris convinced his OKW superiors to let him rekindle the group as part of his Abwehr ('Defence') command, a revived intelligence office so named to appease the Allies in 1921 as to its defensive mandate. Possessing a mindset in which he fought for his country but quietly resisted its present government, Canaris appointed like-minded personnel as he worked to expand Germany's largely decentralized intelligence network.

One of his officers was Dr Theodor von Hippel, who had advocated a highly trained unit, capable of infiltration and sabotage, since joining the Wehrmacht four years previously and the Abwehr two years after that. On 10 October 1939 Canaris appointed him to establish and head up the Abwehr Section II. Sabotage unit. Von Hippel had the necessary experience and drive for the job, having volunteered to serve in World War I under Lettow-Vorbeck in East Africa, one of history's greatest guerilla campaigns, and was a student of Colonel T. E. Lawrence's hit-and-run Arab cavalry tactics against the Turks in Arabia. In just five days, many former members from Battalion Ebbinghaus, Sudetendeutsches Freikorps, which had performed similar duties in 1938 Sudetenland, and returning Abwehr *V-Leute* (*Vertrauensleute*, confidential informants) fresh from the Polish campaign, were formed into what was code-named Bau- und Lehrkompanie (DK) z.b.V. (Construction and Instruction Company (German Company) for special assignment). Officially created on 25 October, it was subsequently renamed Bau-Lehr-Kompanie z.b.V. 800, but the unit's soldiers were popularly known in English as 'Brandenburgers', having been established at the town of Brandenburg an der Havel just west of Berlin. It was organizationally comprised of five sections, including secret intelligence services, counter-intelligence, security sabotage, counter-sabotage, and special duties.

**25 OCTOBER 1939**

**The 'Brandenburger' unit is formed**

Having been awarded the Knight's Cross on 14 September 1942 for his leadership of the Maikop operation, Oberleutnant Adrian von Fölkersam is shown interrogating Soviet prisoners. (Archiv M. Heinz)

On 23 November 1939, two additional companies were created. On 15 December, the formation was renamed Bau-Lehr-Bataillon z.b.V. 800, and on 24 December 1939 the 'Brandenburger' name was first used. With a fourth company integrated into this multilingual and multicultural formation on 10 January 1940, the formation comprised 1st Company (Balt, Russian), 2nd Company (English, Portuguese, former German African colonial), 3rd Company (Sudeten Germans who spoke Czech, Slovak, and Ruthenian), and 4th Company (Polish, Belarusian, Russian, and Ukrainian). A V-Leute company was integrated with 1st Company, and Interpreter companies were added in spring 1940. Due to this expansion, on 1 June the entire unit was again redesignated Lehr-Regiment Brandenburg z.b.V. 800. Trained to conduct a variety of commando-style, *kleinkrieg* (guerrilla) missions, other companies soon followed, including Signals (January 1941), 17th Special, and Training (April 1941), and Light Engineer (February 1942, from 4th Company).

Recruitment into the Brandenburgers, like that of the Abwehr, was strictly based on volunteers, with the understanding that unlike in the regular armed forces, members could refuse to participate in any mission without consequences. As in the event of capture they could be treated as spies, they could not be commanded to operate outside the applicable laws of war, even if the Soviet Union did not officially recognize these, having not signed the Geneva Convention of 1929. Candidates had to be motivated, adventurous, physically fit, and show an aptitude for improvization, marksmanship, self-control, foreign customs and cultures, and be fluent in at least one additional language. As the war expanded, *Volksdeutsche* from occupied Europe and areas slated to be captured were recruited, and as the Brandenburgers' reputation for conducting daring, dangerous missions spread, regular army soldiers increasingly applied to what they viewed as an elite formation as well.

The *Generalfeldzeugmeister-Kaserne* (barracks) in Brandenburg an der Havel. (Archiv M. Heinz)

As part of German combat operations in the west, starting in April 1940, Brandenburger units participated in a variety of covert missions in support of conventional forces. In Denmark, they secured primary roads and river crossings near the border (in civilian dress) and via glider at the Great Belt Bridge (in Danish uniforms), and during the following month assisted Alpine units in Norway, as well as securing bridges in Holland and similar structures in Belgium to prevent the low-lying area from being flooded. Well suited for reconnaissance duties and supporting offensive operations, as the Germans turned eastward in 1941 the Brandenburgers remained an important complement to traditional operations in the Balkans and Yugoslavia, and even conducted clandestine missions in areas as distant as Persia, Afghanistan, India, and North Africa.

Initial Brandenburger training was conducted at Abwehr II's Kampfschule Quenzgut, an estate along the Quenzsees, a lake just west of Brandenburg. Having been established on 28 October 1941, the school had since been isolated from the outside world, where Brandenburgers learned to exemplify their credo of 'seeing without being seen'. Instruction included languages, swimming, the customs and traditions of potential mission regions, secret messaging, small-unit and individual combat techniques, fieldcraft, explosives and sabotage, terrain and map reading (day and night), long-range scouting, infiltration, and recognition of enemy uniforms, ranks, vehicles, and weapons. The optimal recruit tended to be college-educated and had had civilian occupations before the war, as such a person possessed a degree of maturity, experience, and self-sufficiency, and was often strong-willed, self-confident, and a nonconformist.

# INITIAL STRATEGY

*Kampfgruppe* elements of 25th Panzer Regiment (part of 3. Panzergruppe, Heeresgruppe Mitte), having just crossed the 1939 Soviet–German border on 22 June 1941. By early afternoon, this armoured column of several Panzer 38(t)s (towing fuel trailers), followed by a Panzer IV, Panzer 38(t), and Panzer II, would secure vital bridges over the Memel River at Olita. (NARA)

## Operation *Barbarossa*

Having fought with the Russians against Napoleon's ill-fated 1812 invasion, Prussian Lieutenant-Colonel Karl von Clausewitz commented that his adversary's failure was not due to operational overreach, but rather that the region 'could be subdued only by its own weakness and by the effects of internal dissension'. At the end of 1941, Axis forces found themselves in a similar situation. Having advanced 1,000km into the Soviet Union over the previous six months, but unable to capture Leningrad and Moscow or hold Rostov-on-Don, they now had to maintain a 2,800km front line from near Murmansk on the Arctic Ocean to Taganrog on the Sea of Azov.

A repeat of the previous world war, in which Germany had inflicted such battlefield losses against Imperial Russia that it had triggered its economic and military collapse and prompted a revolution that removed the nation from the conflict, was not immediately in the offing. Bitterly cold weather and Soviet reserves that had been opportunistically transferred to the Moscow sector from the Far East enabled the Red Army to defend its country's administrative and political centre and stabilize the front. With both sides having suffered considerable losses in men and materiel during the summer and fall, the resulting counter-attack proved unable to capitalize on its initial success and emulate Tsarist Russia's success in rebuffing Napoleon's 'Grand Army'.

Although the Germans maintained superiority in command and control, doctrine, and technology, their battlefield attrition and a lack of opportunities for rest, refitting, and reorganization similarly degraded their combat effectiveness. An ever-lengthening logistics chain was harassed by partisans and those enemy forces that had been bypassed, and severe manpower, materiel, and fuel shortages conspired to hamper further offensive operations for the foreseeable future.

## The Eastern Front in 1942

Although many German senior commanders favoured moving to a defensive stance along the Eastern Front for up to a year to regain their strength, Hitler would have none of it. Maintaining his incorrect assumption that the Red Army was on the verge of collapse, he ordered Chief of the General Staff, Generaloberst Franz Halder, to prepare for a spring invasion towards the Don and Volga rivers and into the Caucasus to secure the facilities that produced nearly 95 per cent of the enemy's oil. Once controlled, the southern sector could serve as a springboard from which the Germans could renew their effort to encircle Moscow, this time from the south and east. Hitler's delusions of Soviet weakness and German operational capabilities, however, were soon confronted with reality, much of it of his own making.

In part to maintain popular support and to avoid completely altering the nation's situation to a war economy, domestic military production largely operated as if it were peacetime. Hitler's pre-*Barbarossa* Directive 32 had reduced military asset production for the Army in favour of strengthening the Luftwaffe and Navy for another effort to eliminate Great Britain in 1940, and this necessitated more modest goals for the coming campaigning season in 1942. Instead of using Heeresgruppen Nord (North), Mitte (Centre), and Süd (South), as in 1941, only the latter could be allocated to offensive operations, and even then only at 80 per cent effectiveness compared to the previous year. Pressured to compensate for such deficiencies, Axis Italy, Rumania, and Hungary provided men and materiel as well.

On 5 April 1942, Hitler issued Directive 41, which defined German war aims for 1942 on the Eastern Front, including capturing Leningrad, securing the Crimean Peninsula, and cleaning up partisan-controlled rear areas to better focus on the summer's primary combat operations. As a continuous front line could not be maintained in sectors that had been weakened, he further ordered that indigenous labour construct strong defences at key areas to protect logistics and communications from the Baltic to the Sea of Azov, including the cities of Gatchina, Luga, Pskov, Nevel, Smolensk, Roslavl, Bryansk, Poltava, Dnepropetrovsk, and Melitopol. To make the best use of limited resources the offensive was to be undertaken in three consecutive stages, comprising the capture of Voronezh and a thrust along the Don River, and a coordinating pincer movement east of Rostov-on-Don to encircle and eliminate Marshal Semyon Timoshenko's South-West Front. With their rear thus secured, German spearheads would then encircle and destroy Soviet forces to the south and south-east of Rostov-on-Don, and strike for the coastal ports of Novorossiysk and Tuapse to deprive the Black Sea Fleet of

**22 JUNE 1941**

**Operation *Barbarossa* is launched**

During a training demonstration, a shaped-charge German magnetic mine is detonated against a captured Soviet T-34 Model 1943, which has all steel road wheels, a 'hardedge' turret (minus cupola), and no rear fuel tanks. Introduced in 1940, these simple, rugged vehicles presented an excellent balance of armour, firepower, and mobility, and were produced in considerable numbers during the war. (NARA)

an anchorage, secure the area for German shipping, and establish direct communication with Turkey to assist with a possible invasion of the Middle East and link up with friendly forces advancing from North Africa.

On the anticipated successful conclusion of Operation *Barbarossa*, the Germans planned to establish a Reichskommissariat Kaukasus as a political entity once they had captured the region. Unlike the newly created Reichskommissariat Ostland and Ukraine, and the planned Moskowen and Turkestan, these 'indigenous groups' were initially to govern the North Caucasus as pro-German client states. Tasking his commanders with eliminating the Soviet ability to continue the war, Hitler determined that the large movements of encirclement conducted during the previous year allowed too many enemy formations to escape, and instead pushed for smaller, more numerous encirclement battles.

With little direction from Oberkommando des Heeres (OKH, Army High Command) or insight beyond knowing he would receive an influx of new divisions and that his Heeresgruppe Süd command would eventually be divided during the coming offensive, on 29 April Generalfeldmarschall Fedor von Bock and his staff formulated Directive 1 to implement Directive 41. Tasked with securing the front from Voronezh to the Don and Volga rivers and south into the Caucasus, 68 German and 25 allied divisions along a 725km front were at his disposal. In an effort to direct enemy attention to what was probably a better operational objective, the Germans implemented a disinformation campaign focused on another push to capture Moscow, something the Stavka (Armed Forces High Command) already believed was the most logical enemy option. As part of Operation *Kremlin*, the Germans successfully reinforced this mindset by issuing fake orders and sealed maps of the endeavour, and increased aerial reconnaissance over likely targets. During the May 1942 build-up, German divisions and higher commands were given cover names as part of an effort to confuse enemy intelligence.

The Soviet Union, like Germany, also struggled to produce sufficient fuel to maintain its military in the field. In anticipation of the Caucasus being overrun in late 1941, the Soviets had evacuated or rigged for demolition much of the drilling and related petroleum extraction equipment from around Grozny and Baku to prevent their reuse should they be captured. With Luftwaffe bombers already within range of Azerbaijan, should the Germans choose to destroy these facilities instead, existing fuel rationing would do little to avert a crippling blow to Soviet operational movement. As the Soviets' oil pipelines in the region led east toward the Black Sea and Rostov-on-Don, what was moved north had to be transported on the Volga River on large barges.

Should the Germans take the city of Stalingrad, which lay on the Volga, the Soviets would have to redirect millions of tons of oil east across the Caspian Sea to the Krasnovodsk shore, and then north to the Soviet heartland.

The oil question was becoming crucial for both combatant nations. To emphasize his intention, at a meeting of Heeresgruppe Süd's senior officers at Poltava on 1 June 1942, Hitler stated that 'If I do not get the oil of Maikop and Grozny then I must end this war.' Nearly two weeks later, Halder reported that based on a land forces quartermaster's assessment, fuel for the upcoming summer offensive was only expected to last until mid-September.

By June the Soviet counter-offensives, especially at Izium south of Kharkov, had been checked, and the Red Army subsequently moved to the defensive in operational terms. This concerned German senior commanders in case it indicated an enemy alerted to the coming offensive in the south, originally drawn up on 18 March 1942 as Operation *Siegfried*, and later changed to *Blau*.

A Fieseler Fi-156 'Storch' ('Stork') provides reconnaissance for advancing German forces on 1 July 1941. On 19 June 1942 Major Joachim Reichel (23rd Panzer Division) was carrying a copy of Operation *Blau* on such a plane when it was forced to land behind enemy lines. (NARA)

Such potential threats to security and surprise were only reinforced when on 19 June a Fieseler Fi-156 'Storch' ('Stork') carrying 23rd Panzer Division's 1st Generalstaboffizier (Chief of Staff Operations Division), Major Joachim Reichel, and a copy of Operation *Blau*, strayed over enemy lines and crashed. Faced with the prospect of such intelligence falling into the hands of the enemy and giving them sufficient time in which to respond effectively, Bock attempted to move up the offensive's X-Day. Delays with getting Hitler's consent, and rainy weather and the resulting mud, however, conspired to delay its start.

In the lead-up to Operation *Blau*, the German effort to equip participating formations with adequate amounts of motor transport had fallen short, due to inadequate domestic production, captured vehicles that required a nearly endless variety of replacement parts, and the frequently long distances needed to get to assembly positions. Despite intensive maintenance and repair efforts the spearhead divisions had at most 60 per cent of their organic complement. The supply situation during *Blau's* opening segment appeared satisfactory, with sufficient ammunition and rations available for the second phase (*Blau II*), but petrol, oil, and lubricant reserves would likely be consumed by 15 July unless prioritized, and the continuation of the offensive would be dependent on current shipments. Having participated in *Barbarossa*, and more recently the winter fighting along the Mius River and elsewhere along the Eastern Front, most German formations struggled to rest and recuperate. The near constant Soviet pressure meant German formations were often unable to exit forward combat positions temporarily to rest, replenish, and train, or reposition to other sectors, which reduced their combat effectiveness. Armoured divisions suffered from a shortage of technicians and lorry drivers;

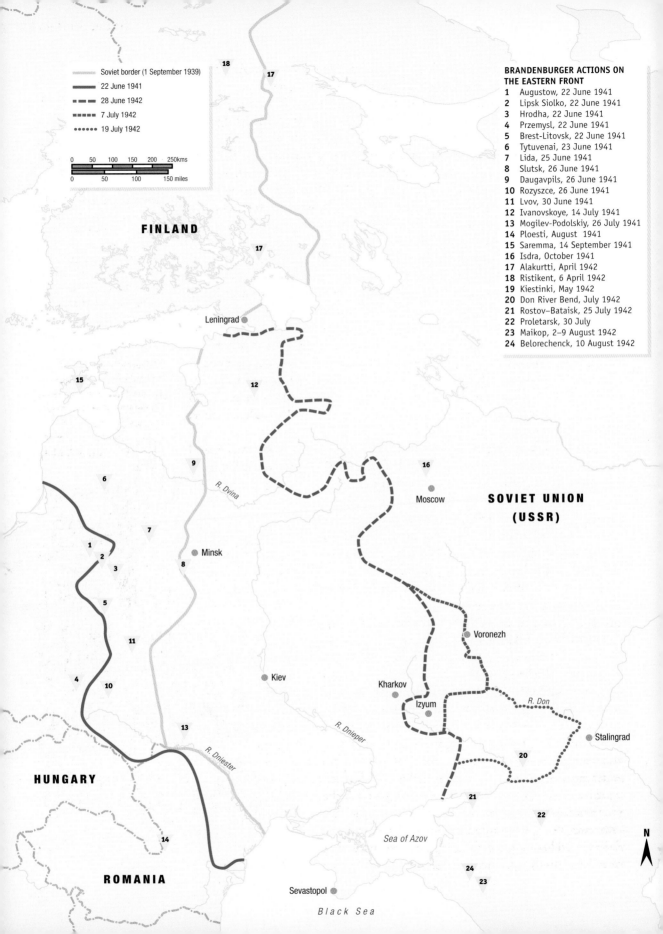

**Soviet border (1 September 1939)**
— 22 June 1941
— — 28 June 1942
— — — 7 July 1942
•••••• 19 July 1942

0   50  100  150  200  250kms
0      50      100     150 miles

FINLAND

**BRANDENBURGER ACTIONS ON
THE EASTERN FRONT**
1  Augustow, 22 June 1941
2  Lipsk Siolko, 22 June 1941
3  Hrodha, 22 June 1941
4  Przemysl, 22 June 1941
5  Brest-Litovsk, 22 June 1941
6  Tytuvenai, 23 June 1941
7  Lida, 25 June 1941
8  Slutsk, 26 June 1941
9  Daugavpils, 26 June 1941
10 Rozyszce, 26 June 1941
11 Lvov, 30 June 1941
12 Ivanovskoye, 14 July 1941
13 Mogilev-Podolskiy, 26 July 1941
14 Ploesti, August  1941
15 Saremma, 14 September 1941
16 Isdra, October 1941
17 Alakurtti, April 1942
18 Ristikent, 6 April 1942
19 Kiestinki, May 1942
20 Don River Bend, July 1942
21 Rostov–Bataisk, 25 July 1942
22 Proletarsk, 30 July
23 Maikop, 2–9 August 1942
24 Belorechenck, 10 August 1942

18

17

17

Leningrad

15

12

9

R. Dvina

6

16

Moscow

**SOVIET UNION
(USSR)**

7

1
2
3

8  Minsk

5

11

Voronezh

Kiev

4

10

Kharkov

Izyum

R. Don

13

R. Dnieper

Stalingrad

R. Dniester

20

HUNGARY

21

22

14

Sea of Azov

24

23

**ROMANIA**

Sevastopol

*Black Sea*

N

and to relieve manpower shortages, Tatar, Caucasian, Georgian, Armenian, and Cossack prisoners were allocated to routine labour duties.

As the time for action approached, an extensive German training programme evolved in the immediate rear areas, with units alternating with auxiliary formations. Such efforts, including the general interest in the men's welfare, translated into a sense of camaraderie among the ranks, where high morale and the inherent value of the individual soldier countered the unceasing efforts of enemy propaganda. During this period, SS Division (Motorized) Wiking focused on using experience gained the previous year, which included assault and shock training in any weather or time of day, while artillery practised rapid firing and barrages against moving targets. Unable to complete its rehabilitation by the start of the offensive, infantry was roughly at half-strength, although it drew additional units as they became available. Armoured units worked on inter-vehicle/unit fire and movement drills, in coordination with artillery, engineers, and Panzergrenadiers, while recovery personnel were instructed in vehicle removal while under fire and in providing ad hoc repairs. Engineers practised rapid mine removal under fire, armour destruction, and demolitions, and imparted these skills to Panzergrenadier personnel. The rear echelon organized a mobile, mechanized supply train that was capable of performing maintenance in a fast war of movement, and military police were given refresher training in traffic control, march discipline, and motor vehicle emergency service.

During this relative lull in the fighting, German observation and intelligence indicated that the Red Army remained active at night in developing fortifications and communication trenches, and in laying mines and other obstructions. Operations had not developed the skills necessary for effective all-arms fighting, and tactics remained unsophisticated, inflexible, and often costly due to the continued practice of employing reckless, massed infantry attacks. Individual soldiers, or small groups, either showed dogged tenacity in combat or were quick to avoid it. Soviet artillery and camouflage improved, and a large amount of flash and sound detection equipment had been distributed, while reconnaissance remained active, and tended to operate in specific sectors. Soviet discipline and morale were buoyed by political commissars, who provided a variety of tasks for enlisted personnel at company and platoon levels, including informing them of the tactical situation, political events, and building confidence in the military's 'unlimited resources', while systematically tearing down the enemy's capabilities and resolve. At higher echelons, staff commissars maintained close observation of officers and lower ranks to best guarantee adherence to orders and the political cause.

**Opposite:**
Having failed to defeat the Red Army during Operation *Barbarossa* (22 June–5 December 1941), by year's end Germany had pushed to the gates of Leningrad in the north and to just west of Rostov. To facilitate the movement of conventional forces, especially during the early frontier battles, specially trained 'Brandenburger' units infiltrated enemy lines to secure bridges and sow confusion until relieved.

A French poster exhorting 'Victory' in 'The Crusade against Bolshevism' in 1942. Should the effort fail, it was stressed that the Soviet Union would overrun most, if not all, of Europe. (Bedos et Cie)

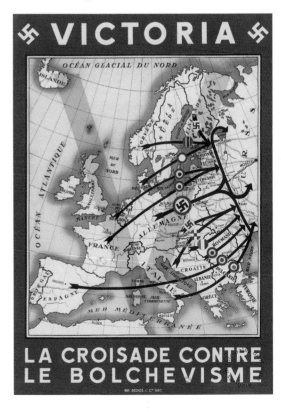

17

Transfer of 200-litre fuel drums from rail to *Nachschubdienste* (supply services) by road transport. Note the structural differences (dual reinforcing or two sets of three ribs). (NARA)

## Operation *Blau*

The offensive would be conducted by Heeresgruppe Weichs, comprising the Second, Fourth Panzer, and Second Hungarian armies, under Generaloberst Maximilian von Weichs. On 28 June, Bock issued the codeword 'Dinkelsbühl' ('Dinosaur'), and the German southern offensive finally launched eastward from around Kharkov, the German forces having repelled the Soviet counter-attack of the second battle of Kharkov in May. In *Blau's* initial phase, the Germans advanced on the important transportation and communication hub of Voronezh along the upper Don River, something the Soviets maintained was a stepping stone for a renewed assault on Tula and Moscow. As such, they were opposed by five Soviet armies, comprising South-western and Southern Fronts respectively under Marshal Timoshenko and Lieutenant-General Rodion Malinovsky, which had recently been considerably depleted during their ill-fated counter-attack near Kharkov. These still succeeded in hampering German progress, however, and in upsetting their carefully conceived timetable and resource allocation. Having flanked the Soviet line, Panzer divisions spearheaded a drive that cascaded southward as Bock carried out a classic series of rolling flank attacks, while also maintaining pressure along the middle Don River. As a result of Reichel's recent crash landing, on 30 June the overall operation's name was changed from *Blau* to *Braunschweig* ('Brunswick'). Although the first campaign stage to capture Voronezh ended around 13 July, it did not receive a name change as did *Blau II* and *Blau III*, to *Clausewitz* and *Dampfhammer* ('Steam Hammer') respectively.

Stalin, the Stavka, and the General Staff continued to believe that the German offensive remained focused on Moscow. With the Soviets readying to resist north-east of Kursk-Voronezh, on 1 July Hitler's staff, the OKW, announced that they had had begun a major offensive 'in the southern and central sectors' of the Eastern Front. Within a week, the Red Army faced a dilemma, as it became increasingly unlikely that Moscow was the goal.

With the South-West Front dislodged between the Donets and Don rivers and pushed into and behind the flank of the neighbouring South Front, the Stavka – for the first time in the war – ordered a strategic retreat. On 6 July, Stalin demanded Voronezh be held at all costs in order to maintain control of the rail line linking Moscow with points south, but the city fell that day. To prevent the Germans from acquiring the Caucasus oil facilities, Stalin tasked his oil industry commissar, Nikolai Baibakov, with securing this vital strategic prize while maintaining supplies to the Red Army, to which the latter replied that the only way was to dismantle the essential equipment and transport it eastwards, continuing to pump and distribute fuel to the front until the last minute, and only then to destroy the oilfields. Stalin approved of the idea, responding that 'if you don't stop the Germans getting our oil, you will be shot, and when we have thrown the invader out, if we cannot restart production we will shoot you again.'

On 7 July, the formation that had been held in reserve since May, *Küstenstab Asow* (Coastal Staff Azov), lost its cover name as it was officially assigned as headquarters for a new Heeresgruppe A under Generalfeldmarschall Wilhelm List, which was to use First Panzer Army to strike into the Caucasus. The following day, Heeresgruppe Süd provided Seventeenth Army and Third Rumanian Army, which were organized as a temporary command, Heeresgruppe Ruoff. To provide for the eastward offensive, Bock's command was redesignated Heeresgruppe B on 9 July. With German forces having captured Sevastopol the previous week after an eight-month siege and secured the Crimea, Ploesti was now safe from Soviet bombers that could otherwise have used the 'Soviet aircraft carrier' (the Crimean peninsula) to deliver attacks. On 11 July, Hitler issued Directive 43, in which Erich von Manstein's Eleventh Army was to cross the Kerch Strait and into the Taman Peninsula by early August. Under the code name *Blücher*,

A portion of the estimated 103,000 Soviet soldiers captured on 14 August 1941 during the German encirclement around Uman. After similarly large numbers of Red Army prisoners taken during *Barbarossa*, including Kiev (665,000), Vyazma-Bryansk (663,000), and Smolensk (310,000), a year later such hauls would pale in comparison. (NARA)

A pair of Luftwaffe Horch Kfz 15 and a Sturmgeschütz III Ausf F8 or G on the Eastern Front. Note the track segments affixed to the assault gun's rear, which imparted a degree of additional armour protection, and the *Winterketten* extensions to lessen the vehicle's ground pressure in soft terrain. (NARA)

the operation was to secure the Black Sea ports of Anapa and Novorossiysk to deprive the enemy of their use, followed by an eastward thrust north of the Caucasus Mountains. If possible, a follow-up attack would push along the coastal highway via Tuapse. The Luftwaffe was to provide the Army with support and logistics, while naval forces in the Black Sea would offer indirect assistance as needed. Consideration was even given to using 22nd Infantry Division in a reprisal of its *Luftlande* (air landing) role when during the 1940 invasion of Holland it acted as a tactical response unit to quickly capture enemy airfields.

With Seventeenth Army having pushed around Rostov-on-Don to the north, stubborn successive Soviet rearguards prompted Hitler to redirect First Panzer Army from supporting Fourth Panzer Army's eastward advance on 13 July to help secure crossings over the Don River to the south-west instead. In addition to the operational and logistic difficulties of securing physically divergent goals, the Germans' limited fuel supplies slowed their advance tempo, as rationing and prioritizing limited vehicle usage and contributed to the Red Army's ability to avoid becoming bypassed and eliminated, a tactic many of Stalin's senior commanders, and British and American advisers, promoted. Three days later, with German forces having overrun a large tract of enemy territory from Voronezh and along the Don River to Rostov-on-Don, Hitler arrived at his Vinnitsa headquarters. Located along a proposed post-war German highway connecting Europe and the Crimean Peninsula, the Führer was also close to the respective command posts of Heeresgruppe B and A west of Poltava and Stalino.

Strong German armour formations from First Panzer Army pushed along the lower course of the Don River, intent on joining Panzer divisions of Fourth Panzer Army south of Millerovo to encircle and destroy Donets Front. Due to the barriers posed by the Donets and Don River tributaries, hilly terrain, and underdeveloped road infrastructure, the deployment was only half completed, and only one pincer was able to move through the large elements of Fifty-First and Thirty-Seventh Soviet armies to the east and south. Underestimating their enemy's ability to retreat faster than they could advance, Fourth Panzer Army became entangled in the fight for Voronezh, which degraded the overall offensive's tempo and enabled Timoshenko to escape to the south-east. As air transport had proven effective in supplementing ground-based logistics during the Norwegian campaign in April 1940 and *Barbarossa* in 1941, the Luftwaffe's Junkers Ju 52 transport fleet flew in some 200 tonnes of fuel per day just to keep Sixth Army moving as it advanced southeast along the Don River, and was now some 100km from the Volga River and Stalingrad. Because several of the overrun airstrips were not near German railheads or established supply routes, construction, supply, and maintenance personnel and equipment often had to be flown into these areas to get them operational.

By 19 July, elements of Fourth Panzer Army had already reached the Don River's north bank, with Grossdeutschland and 24th Panzer Division respectively some 100 and 200km east of Rostov-on-Don. Within the enclosing ring, the Soviet Ninth, Twelfth, Eighteenth, Thirty-Seventh, and Fifty-Sixth armies were being pushed back on the waterway and into the city. Over the next few days, Heeresgruppe A initiated a cascading movement that worked to steadily isolate Rostov-on-Don, using First Panzer Army in a wide clockwise movement on List's left, while Heeresgruppe Ruoff would conduct a direct assault on the inside. Up to this point, the rapid German operational tempo had surprised its largely disorganized adversary, which spun the situation as an intentional effort to draw them into a trap. While superficially the campaign was progressing well, except for encircling large Soviet formations around Izium and later Millerovo, subsequent prisoner hauls were disappointing. Regardless, Hitler maintained that the uncoordinated Soviet retreat indicated effective resistance was coming to an end.

# THE PLAN

## The war for oil

Hitler had long known that the Soviets would not relinquish their oilfields without a fight, and would certainly not let them fall into German hands intact. A captured copy of Marshal Timoshenko's secret December 1941 speech to the Soviet Supreme Defence Council recorded his belief that possession of the oilfields was even more important than the security of the capital. He emphasized that even if the Germans captured Moscow they would gain little more than additional winter shelter; if necessary, the Soviets would destroy anything useful to the enemy. Instead, the real war-deciding fight would be over oil, and all that was needed to ultimately triumph was to 'make Germany increase her oil consumption, and to keep the German armies out of the Caucasus'.

In 1941, over 93 per cent of all Soviet oil and fuel supplies passed through the Caucasus, including 59 per cent through Baku and Batum, and 28 per cent through the Chechnyan capital of Grozny, which together provided some 91 per cent of the USSR's refining needs. Should the Soviet strategic oil reserves at Malgobek, Kievskoe, and Maikop be destroyed rather than taken intact, the Germans would have to rely on supplies from distant Rumania, which alone had the surplus storage capacity to hold such large quantities of additional crude. With the Soviets having practised 'scorched earth' tactics to deny as much as possible to the advancing Germans, it stood to reason that

A postcard of Baku in 1914 showing holding tanks and refining facilities; it was known as the 'Black City' due to the oily atmosphere that permeated the area. (PD)

Черный городъ.
Ville noire.

Баку — Bakou.

they would certainly attempt to destroy or damage the numerous wells, pipelines, storage tanks, refineries, and surrounding road and rail infrastructure if similarly threatened with capture.

## Technical challenges

The Germans had equally few doubts about the critical importance of taking the Soviet oilfields. The German Army alone required 5,000 to 6,000 tons of oil per day in addition to the needs of the Luftwaffe, Kriegsmarine, and Germany's general transportation. During the planning for Operation *Barbarossa*, in spring 1941, OKW had established a specially trained and equipped Petroleum Detachment Caucasus near Berlin at Templin. This engineering unit would follow front-line formations to quickly re-establish drilling, storage, and refining once such assets were captured. An advance into the Caucasus had originally been planned for 1941, but had to be postponed until the following year.

By 20 December 1941, the oilfield engineers had a strength of roughly 5,400 German technicians and an equal number of Soviet prisoners of war and civilian forced labourers. Now under the command of a Luftwaffe Generalmajor, Erich Homberg, they were allocated 1,142 vehicles and six aircraft with which to perform their duties. Once the oilfields were seized, the Germans optimistically estimated that it would take less than a year to get the Maikop oil wells to produce one million tons annually (50 per cent of Soviet peacetime production) sometime in 1942, while Grozny, and especially Baku's 20 million annual tons, were hoped to produce some 120,000 tons a month starting in mid-1943. It was estimated that 600 drilling installations were needed to compensate for the 836 less efficient Soviet equivalents, but German industry could presently only provide 75 rigs. Although dismantling facilities in occupied countries, especially France, and relocating them east would help to compensate, the Germans still lacked the necessary numbers of drilling and reconstruction experts and sufficient transportation, which was estimated as 300 trains rolling stock.

## Brandenburgers in *Barbarossa*

During Operation *Barbarossa*, the largest military invasion in history, the Brandenburger groups had played a crucial role in getting German armoured and mechanized forces through the border zone by securing bridges, scouting, and impeding enemy efforts to organize at critical locations. First Battalion was also assigned to protecting ethnic Germans, while 2nd and 3rd battalions conducted anti-partisan operations. Having suffered high officer and NCO casualties, on 15 August 1941 nearly all of the regiment's battalions were withdrawn from combat operations in the east and returned to their respective bases at Brandenburg an der Havel, Baden, Austria, and Düren. Under the new regimental commander, Oberst Paul Hähling von Lanzenauer, the units were strengthened and instructed in recent lessons learned. At year's end a fourth battalion was created, and the former commander of 1st Battalion, Major Friedrich Heinz, was ordered to establish an Abwehr *Truppenuebungsplatz* (troop training area) on the existing training grounds

**WINTER 1941**

**Germans fail to take Moscow; planning begins for 1942 operations**

## TBM ORGANIZATION

On 29 March 1942 the head of the OKW's Wehrwirtschafts und Rüstungsamt (War Economy and Armaments Office) expanded the formation, and changed its name three days later to Technische Brigade Mineralöl (TBM, Technical Petroleum Brigade). However, infighting among those with a stake in the matter – OKW, Reichswirtschaftsministerium (Reich Economics Ministry), Reich Ministry for Armaments and Munitions, Göring's ongoing 'Four Year Plan' Office, Ostministerium (Reich Ministry for the Occupied Eastern Territories), and OKH – hindered the accumulation of the necessary 2,800 drilling experts needed for the unit as each vied for such resources.

After basic military training and a stint in the Rumanian oil region of Ploesti to gain practical experience, TBM members were allocated their equipment, much of which had been confiscated from occupied France. This included 100 deep drilling machines, 225 conveyors, and ten portable distillation plants. Transportation to the Eastern Front was conducted by rail to the Black Sea, from where ferries took the material to Berdyansk, some 75km from Mariupol, along the Sea of Azov's north shore.

- Technical Petroleum Brigade (5,400)
- Command and Staff (150)
- Specialist Battalions
- I Drilling, II Processing, III Transport (600)
- Technical Battalions (A/11 and B/33) (1,800), a paramilitary force that included a staff, three technical companies, and platoon-sized radio, surgical, security, etc.
- Transmissions (100)
- Company Transport (120)
- Heavy Transportation Unit (150)

- Battalion Gas Technology (800)
- Technical Water Battalion (800)
- Organization Todt (500)
- DCA 15 and 42 (300)
- Field Hospital (80)

More than two months after the Germans captured Maikop, 3rd Petroleum Brigade has nearly completed construction of a 40m-tall derrick some 50km to the south-west near Neftegorsk ('Oil City') on 16 October 1942. Note the structure's elevated, concrete pylon base and its crewmen. (NARA)

**1 APRIL 1942**

**Technical Petroleum Brigade formed**

at the eastern German town of Meseritz. By March 1942 the Germans had suffered their first million casualties on the Eastern Front, and were preparing for a renewed summer offensive that would once again require Brandenburgers to offer the best chance of success.

Based on the lessons learned during *Barbarossa* and elsewhere, on 26 June 1942, the head of Abwehr II issued Report No. 1509/42 gKdos (*geheime Kommandosache*), which stressed several guidelines for future operations. Brandenburger formations were best employed as part of offensive actions, in which they operated behind enemy lines, ahead of German armoured and motorized formations. When situations moved to the defensive, they were to be pulled from the front in order to receive training in the most recent combat methods, and for refurbishment. Although the Brandenburgers' primary combat unit was the company, the entire regiment could also be allocated to a mission, which should only be used in temporary or emergency contingencies in order to preserve these specialists. In the field, Lehr-Regiment Brandenburg z.b.V 800 was to be attached to army groups and armies, and a Brandenburger company was not to assist more than one division at a time. When used as companies or larger formations, a liaison officer was to be provided to coordinate with the army formations to which they were attached.

## An unconventional plan

Operation *Edelweiss*, the plan to take the Caucasus and their oilfields, would be launched in July 1942. However, success would depend not only on the oil engineers' skills, but also on the ability of German forces to take the oilfields and equipment before the Soviets destroyed them. Conventional forces would be unable to advance the hundreds of kilometres between the Don River and the Western Caucasus Mountains fast enough to capture the enemy's oil assets intact, and an airborne option would likely be expected. An unconventional solution was required.

To provide unconventional assets for securing or sabotaging key assets in the Caucasus and to assist friendly ground operations, elements of 1st and 2nd Brandenburger battalions had been allocated to the upcoming campaign. As a component of *Blücher*, Lanzenauer prepared his command for a variety of missions in the region, including securing the geographically closest oil facilities near Maikop, and destroying the Krasnodar–Kropotkin–Tikhoretsk rail lines and surrounding bridges to isolate the Kuban Peninsula. The regiment's refurbished 4th (Light Engineer) Company would also sabotage Black Sea harbour and coastal installations to hamper the ingress of enemy reinforcements, and disrupt their naval logistics and operations.

Leutnant Adrian Freiherr (Baron) von Fölkersam was the Brandenburger officer tasked with seizing the Maikop oil facilities. The mission would require his unit to infiltrate deep behind enemy lines, remain in the area for roughly a week, and secure as much of the area's oil extraction, refining, and storage assets as possible until conventional forces arrived, while also facilitating the push into the Western Caucasus Mountains toward Tuapse on the Black Sea coast. Like his fellow Brandenburger officers, he had control over tactical planning.

To best ensure mission success and minimize enemy suspicion, von Fölkersam decided that the

**5 APRIL 1942**

**Hitler lays out main elements of Operation *Blau***

Oberst Paul Hähling von Lanzenauer (left) and Major Friedrich Heinz (centre) conversing with a third officer at the Generalfeldzeugmeister-Kaserne. (Archiv M. Heinz)

ideal cover would be to go behind the lines disguised as an NKVD unit – Stalin's dreaded security force, which could mete out summary executions as it saw fit to maintain order and discipline. To reduce unanticipated variables, eliminate obstacles, and promote rapid action and success, simplicity and a limited number of objectives were paramount. Therefore the mission was to be a ground insertion, once an opportunity south of the Don River presented itself. Von Fölkersam's soldiers were mostly men from the Baltic states who spoke fluent Russian, and personally selected Sudeten Germans.

Known for his battlefield improvisation, Fölkersam was well suited to lead such a mission, having previously led several operations into the Soviet rear alongside independence-minded Balts. Staunchly anti-Soviet, his Balts and Sudeten Germans were personally motivated to see the Maikop mission through successfully. He also needed to promote a sense of purpose that focused the men on thoroughly understanding objectives at each phase, and a personal commitment to accomplish the job. This reduced extraneous objectives, isolated the necessary intelligence, tailored requirements, and ensured the unit remained mission-centred. Surprise, speed, deception, timing, and audacity were paramount during the execution phase, as the Brandenburgers had historically acted against a prepared enemy. For this operation, in which the veteran participants had previously fought together, 62 Brandenburgers were to undertake the long-range Maikop mission, while 24 members were to make a shorter-range effort to secure the bridge over the Belaya River, some 10km downstream.

**Left:**
Similar to the pipelines that connected the Caucasus oil-producing centres such as Baku, Grozny, and Maikop with the Black Sea and north through Rostov-on-Don, this section ran between Alexandria and Kirovograd (Ukraine) seen here on 4 September 1941. (NARA)

**Right:**
During the oil extraction process, flare stacks were used to burn off undesired natural gas that accompanied the liquid. (NARA)

## Training for the mission

In anticipation of further unconventional operations on the Eastern Front, in July 1941 the Germans had begun to establish commando training schools that were closer to that theatre. At one such facility in East Prussia, Fölkersam tried to provide the most realistic training possible for his men. Subjecting them to a painstaking, totally immersive environment, Brandenburger officers used captured manuals and other resources to replicate NKVD training, discipline, procedures, attitudes, and customs, as well as what lower-ranking personnel had learned during their related schooling where they were exposed to a combination of political indoctrination, military training, and instruction in criminal law and procedure, investigation, intelligence, and counter-intelligence. To be as culturally accurate as possible, the men were versed in proper slang, drank copious amounts to develop their alcohol tolerance so that they could blend into whatever social situations might arise, and practised with the types of enemy weapons, equipment, and vehicles that might be expected. They spoke Russian at all times and assumed their new roles, including wearing their cover uniforms. With the Balts having suffered under nearly two years of harsh Soviet occupation, and everyone having witnessed the results of NKVD atrocities committed against *Volksdeutsche*, Polish, Latvian, and other political prisoners at Hronda, Lvov, and elsewhere during *Barbarossa*'s early stages, many were loath to comply with the latter.

In infiltrating such an environment, the Brandenburgers practised the correct manner in which to address superiors and peers, and the condescending way they generally dealt with subordinates, regular army soldiers, and civilians, where the most minor offense or hint of disrespect could result in a summary execution. To best emulate such personnel, constant repetition and rehearsal attempted to eliminate character inconsistencies and reduce situational excitement when conducting an operation by making interacting with the enemy automatic and natural. It also honed individual and unit skills and performance, and exposed weaknesses.

Throughout the late 1930s Soviet authorities had increasingly expressed concern about the possibility of 'fifth columnists' operating inside their borders, as indicated by NKVD Resolution No. 00439 on 25 July 1937 that stated 'the German General Staff and the Gestapo in wide measures are organizing espionage and sabotage work … utilizing for this goal specially placed cadres of German extraction.' By mid-1938, propaganda and paranoia evolved into an almost pathological distrust of foreigners, which promoted an aggressive and intrusive campaign to root out, capture, or kill potential spies, subversives, and generally poison the everyday lives of citizens. Perhaps the most focused Soviet and NKVD efforts were directed at the Caucasus, which was seen as vital to its national security interests. With an enemy expecting an attack, Fölkersam's concern was not with concealing his upcoming mission, but rather with timing his arrival in Maikop to minimize his exposure to the enemy, and to a lesser degree accomplishing an undetected insertion.

## Operating behind the lines

During missions behind enemy lines, Brandenburgers wore one of three uniform combinations. A *Halbtarnung* (half camouflage) comprised an enemy uniform that was worn over their official uniform, with the former being removed prior to combat. *Volltarnung* (full camouflage) meant that only civilian clothes or the enemy's uniform was worn. *Mischtarnung* (mixed camouflage) indicated that some Brandenburgers would wear enemy uniforms, with others in proper German uniforms – generally to give the appearance of troops escorting prisoners or deserters. As with other nations, the Brandenburgers thus occasionally waived the protection granted by the Hague Regulations, as such protections only applied when they were subject to a central authority, wore a badge or a uniform, openly carried arms, and abided by the prescribed laws and customs of war.

In theory, should a Brandenburger be captured masquerading in an enemy uniform, he would be considered a non-combatant and not entitled to protection as a legitimate prisoner of war. As such, Brandenburgers would generally be subjected to Articles 29 and 30 of the Land Warfare Convention, regarded as a spy and, in accordance with the customary international laws of war, summarily executed. Should such a soldier operate behind enemy lines, return to friendly positions, and then be captured, he was to be treated as a legitimate prisoner of war under Article 31; in other words he could not be prosecuted because of past espionage activity.

## The Brandenburgers' opponents

With the NKVD having reunited with the People's Commissariat for State Security (NKGB) on 20 July 1941, and with military counter-intelligence the following January, its power and influence increased considerably. The organization was the Communist Party's primary support mechanism. Although members were commensurately rewarded for services rendered, the organization was often difficult to control, as it tended to emancipate itself from external controls and had an interest in preserving the conditions of emergency on which the growth of its power depended. Adding to this sense of extralegal entitlement and the fact that NKVD ranks were the equivalent of a higher Army rank, new recruits were predominantly drawn from trusted Party members who were assigned NKVD duties by the cadre sections of the Secretariat of the Party Central Committee and lower Party organs.

An air-dropped propaganda leaflet, 'The Precious Liquid of Maikop', used ominous imagery including caricatures and Hitler phrases to demoralize German efforts in the Caucasus. (Moscow 1942)

## THE NKVD IN THE CAUCASUS

Although the southern Caucasus region had largely avoided Stalin's forced collectivization programme in 1929 and thus a catastrophic famine like the one that struck the Ukraine and other regions, its tribal population had long resisted amalgamation into the Soviet Union. To bring the region to heel, Stalin made the intelligent yet ruthless Georgian secret police chief, Lavrenti Beria, the first Party Secretary of the Transcaucasian Federation. He initiated a campaign of terror to exterminate the region's intelligentsia and resistance, a policy he maintained nationally after being made head of the NKVD in 1938. Buoyed by the Finnish defence of their homeland against the Red Army during the 1939 Winter War, an independence-minded Chechen guerrilla movement under Khasan Israilov rose up against Moscow. Following the German invasion of the Soviet Union three years later, thousands of Chechens and Ingush joined the Red Army, but many in the Caucasian region, which was historically anti-Russian and anti-Soviet and predominantly Islamic, exploited Moscow's distraction to push for autonomy. In February 1942, another Chechen insurgent group under Maribek Sheripov occupied the mountainous region south-west of Vhechnya-Ingushetia and joined Izrailov, which gave the insurgents control over a large stretch of rugged territory on which they formed a provisional government.

Unwilling to let such events take root, on 18 September 1941 Beria, as Minister of Internal Affairs and NKVD head, signed command No. 001171 to liquidate what he classified as terrorist groups. Initially, local NKVD forces were to conduct these counter-terrorist actions, but as many had familial connections with these groups the effort garnered few successes, since the insurgents simply dissolved when met with strength. The Soviet Union's vast territory dissipated its security forces, and although secessionist movements along the Volga River and in Central Asia were also a cause for concern, the Caucasus, with its valuable oil production and manufacturing assets, made it paramount that Moscow maintain control over as much of the region as possible. As the Germans readied to push into the Caucasus in July 1942, the Chechen and Ingush groups had no desire to trade one 'colonizer' for another, although they claimed that the Germans would be welcomed as guests, if they recognized their independence, a sentiment the attacker looked to leverage.

In the months leading up to the Caucasus fighting, the Abwehr had recruited hundreds of prisoners from throughout the region and trained them to operate behind enemy lines to destabilize communications and transport, as well as to make contact with the pro-independence tribes in the Karachai and Kabardin-Balkar Autonomous Regions and Chechnya-Ingshetia. As head of the Otsministerium's Caucasus division, Gerhard von Mende pioneered the establishment of committees that worked to re-employ the nearly one million Russian and non-Russian prisoners that had volunteered to fight for the Germans. With Hitler's consent, in autumn 1941, the Abwehr created two special-purpose battalions comprised of soldiers from the more rebellious Caucasus and Central Asia. Once in the field they were to assist German efforts and to organize anti-Soviet uprisings behind the lines, and help divide the people from their government and draw them to the German cause.

Tasked with maintaining order and security with all possible vigilance, they predominantly maintained a presence behind the Soviet front lines, which comprised a deep, fluctuating, and potentially deadly 'prohibited zone' several kilometres behind the front lines. Manning a maze of checkpoints, they aggressively searched for forged identification papers, deserters, malingerers, and other potential threats. The Brandenburgers needed to act this part while operating in a tense, alien environment where any deviation from accepted NKVD protocols could mean immediate exposure, torture, and death not for just them, but their comrades.

# THE RAID

## The Caucasus campaign

Having spent the previous several weeks securing Voronezh and pushing south-east along the Don River bend, by 20 July German forces were making steady progress towards their operationally divergent goals to the east and south. Although many senior commanders had expressed concern about the feasibility of completing the assigned missions with the manpower and resources (especially fuel) available, Hitler would have none of it, believing instead that the enemy's southern theatre was on the verge of collapse. Should Heeresgruppe Süd secure the lower Volga River, it would effectively isolate the Caucasus and cover the rear of the forces, which could then focus

A German Army 1st Section Light Telephone Kfz 15 from a Signal Platoon/ Detachment on 15 July 1942. The *Gefreiter* (lance corporal, far right) sports the basic signals qualification patch. (NARA)

on taking Rostov-on-Don in a wide clockwise offensive designed to push to the Sea of Azov and trap the majority of Soviet defenders. Once Seventeenth Army completed its interior push, what few Soviet formations then remained in the North Caucasus would be caught between a rapid First Panzer Army drive from the north, and a festering Islamic revolution behind them in the south. Once the Germans captured Grozny and Baku, even if the Soviets destroyed the oil production facilities, their loss would almost assuredly eliminate Stalin's ability to continue the war beyond a few months.

To best address various battlefield situations, a German corps' attached armour, infantry, artillery, and engineer formations were tactically organized as a *kampfgruppe* (battle group); smaller groupings such as divisions and regiments were organized likewise. On 15 July 1942, Seventeenth Army was temporarily allocated two such commands in addition to its 4th, 11th, and 52nd Army Corps. General der Panzertruppen Friedrich Kirchner's 57th Panzer Corps (13th Panzer Division and Wiking) comprised Ruoff's main strike force, while General der Infanterie Wilhelm Wetzel's 5th Army Corps (9th, 198th, and Slovak fast infantry divisions) was similarly designated '*zur Verfügung*' ('available for duty') and covered the left flank. The remaining corps, 49th Gebirgskorps (Mountain Corps) (298th, 73rd, and 125th infantry divisions), occupied forward positions north of the Sea of Azov, where they would open paths for follow-on armour. In concert, First Panzer Army's 3rd Panzer Corps (14th and 22nd Panzer divisions) continued to advance on Rostov-on-Don from the north-east, with the combined effort designed to trap as much of the Soviet South and South-West Fronts as possible before they could cross the Don River. With German forces having passed *Clausewitz*'s southern phase line running through Millerovo, and their progress toward the Volga River and Stalingrad generally on schedule, adhering to the *Dampfhammer* stage was made unnecessary, as the focus moved to the North Caucasus.

With minimal Soviet air activity in the targeted sector, two days before the 21 July attack, 8th Fliegerkorps (Air Corps) under Generalleutnant Martin Fiebig achieved regional aerial supremacy, and was thus able to operate regular medium bomber sorties to soften known and suspected enemy positions with little interference. As the need for fighter escorts was thus largely negated, these assets could be reallocated to more threatened sectors. As Rostov-on-Don needed to be taken quickly, and the Don River bridges captured intact to best ensure the subsequent encirclement and destruction of enemy forces before they could withdraw into the North Caucasus, Brandenburgers were brought forward.

With Kirchner having issued final attack orders 11 hours previously, at 0330 on 21 July, 298th and 73rd Infantry Division artillery initiated a half-hour barrage that targeted the Soviet 30th Rifle Division and other formations anchoring Fifty-Sixth Army's left against the Sea of Azov. German engineers followed up by hurriedly clearing paths through Soviet barbed wire and minefields. Realizing that the near absence of enemy air interdiction and inconsistent resistance could not always be expected, the need for specialist armoured vehicles to undertake such hazardous tasks was

## BRANDENBURGER ORGANIZATION

On 9 May 1942, Brandenburger forces in the Caucasus were allocated to 3.Generalstaboffizier (General Staff Officer) Ic (Chief Intelligence Officer) of Seventeenth Army. With much of Lehr-Regiment Brandenburg z.b.V 800 having spent the previous several months at their German, Austrian, and other facilities, individual companies began arriving in-theatre between 10 and 12 July. One week later 3rd Battalion moved to Stalino, with 10th and 12th companies continuing to Rovenki, near Voronezh, while the regimental commander Oberst Paul Hähling von Lanzenauer and his staff moved to Rovenki and later Stalino.

- Lehr-Regiment Brandenburg z.b.V 800 (July 1942)
- HQ (Brandenburg an der Havel) (Oberst Paul Hähling von Lanzenauer) (Leutnant, Adjutant Staff, Adrian von Fölkersam)
- 1st Battalion (Brandenburg an der Havel) (Hauptmann Wilhelm Walther)
- 1st Company (Oberleutnant Fritz Babuke)
- 2nd Company (Oberleutnant Helmut Pinkert)
- 3rd Company (Oberleutnant Werner John)
- 4th Company (light engineer) (Oberleutnant Hermann Kürschner)
- 2nd Battalion (Baden-Unterwaltersdorf) (Major Dr Paul Jacobi)
- 5th Company (Hauptmann Johann Karl Fürchtegott Zülch)
- 6th Company (Oberleutnant der Reserve Hans-Gerhard Bansen)
- 7th Company (Oberleutnant Karl-Heinz Österwitz)
- 8th Company (Hauptmann der Reserve Siegfried Grabert/ Leutnant Ernst Prochaska)
- 3rd Battalion (Düren) (Hauptmann F. Jacobi)
- 9th Company (Oberleutnant Dr Gottfried Kniesche)
- 10th Company (Leutnant Kriegsheim)
- 11th Company
- 12th Company (Oberleutnant Schader)
- 15th Company (light) (Leutnant Trommsdorff)
- 4th Battalion
- 13th (Special), 14th (Replacement Training), 16th, 17th (Special) Companies
- Künstjager Company
- Signals Battalion (1st–3rd Companies)

paramount. In response to the present and seemingly inexorable German advance Malinovsky initiated a fighting withdrawal to the Don River, while his subordinate, Viktor Tsyganov, having defended the Rostov-on-Don area eight months before, prepared his Fifty-Sixth Army to reprise the role.

As 298th and 73rd Infantry Divisions advanced eastward along the coast to seize the high ground beyond Sambek, 125th Infantry Division pushed ahead on their left to help create penetrations through which Group Kirchner's armoured formations would pass. Because the exposed, open terrain made ground reconnaissance hazardous, Junkers Ju 87 'Stuka' dive-bombers offered coordinated 'flying artillery' support to promote a rapid ground attack tempo. Having defended a predominantly static sector since the previous November, Wiking was eager for a war of movement as it, and 13th Panzer Division, moved up to exploit the gaps opened by their supporting infantry.

Wiking had been created in December 1940 as the first Waffen-SS division comprised of non-Germans. Now, its Westland (Dutch and Flemish) Motorized Infantry Regiment had given its vehicles to Germania (ethnic Germans) and Nordland (Danes, Norwegians, and Swedes) to provide for three *kampfgruppen* under SS-Sturmbannführer August Dieckmann (I./Germania), SS-Hauptsturmführer Arnold Stoffers (SS-Freiwilligen-Legion 'Flandern') and SS-Hauptsturmführer Rüdiger Weitzdörfer (II./Nordland). With 73rd Infantry Division pushing frontally against heavy resistance,

**28 JUNE 1942**

Operation *Blau* is launched

Dieckmann skirted the area to the north-east of the Tuzlov River to maintain the drive across the broad plateau and numerous, high-banked *balkas* (ravines) between it and the Mius before turning back toward Rostov-on-Don.

## The battle for Rostov-on-Don

At daybreak the massed air power of 8th Air Corps bombed forward enemy defences and artillery positions between the Kolmyskaya River and the dry creek running through Krym. Simultaneously, Kirchner's *kampfgruppen* left their forward assembly positions and began their thrust on Rostov-on-Don, with air-to-ground communication coordinated by radio through Luftwaffe liaisons travelling in armoured halftracks. As Wiking and 13th Panzer Division fought through the city's outer defensive ring and integrated anti-tank ditch, supporting artillery helped pin the defenders, many of whom were demoralized from the recent aerial bombing. This allowed engineers to advance to quickly construct temporary bridges over the obstruction. Specially trained for assault roles, I./Germania Panzergrenadiers followed closely behind their armoured spearheads toward the south, and within an hour had pushed beyond Rostov-on-Don's outermost defences.

With Wiking making progress, Generalmajor Traugott Heer's 13th Panzer Division began its attack just to the north at 0945. Having helped capture the city the year before, members of the latter formation were familiar with the area through which its *kampfgruppen*, formed around 66th and 83rd Panzergrenadier regiments, now advanced. After a midday break from the soaring temperatures, 13th Panzer Division pushed toward Sultan Sali along the Stalino–Rostov-on-Don road, as 125th Infantry Division passed Aleksandrovka and moved up on its left. On Heer's right, Wiking had similarly swung north of the most direct and heavily defended route into Rostov-on-Don, and although the deviation put the unit behind schedule, the flanking move minimized losses at a time when every resource was needed to maintain the formation's strength and endurance. With the Soviet defence increasingly uncoordinated, German armour negotiated numerous minefields and emplaced flamethrowers, as they overran the dissolving enemy remnants.

That night, Gruppe Wetzel had largely achieved its day's objectives, having penetrated Rostov-on-Don's outer defences, and had arrived at the second of the city's three main defensive rings. Having travelled 30km since starting operations, Wiking and 13th Panzer Division were now just 15km from the city's western edge. To assist in capturing the area's only crossing of the 300–400m-wide Don River that was capable of taking large amounts of

**22 JULY 1942**

**German forces enter Rostov-on-Don**

On 22 July 1942, Wiking penetrated Rostov's outer defensive line, which had been incorporated into this *balka* north-west of Krym. (Youriy Mishurin)

vehicle and personnel traffic, Oberleutnant Siegfried Grabert's 8./II Brandenburg Battalion was attached to the formation, which was already making for the railway bridge and causeway leading to Bataisk and the firm terrain of the North Caucasus beyond.

As German forces advanced on Rostov-on-Don's middle defensive line early on 22 July, Luftwaffe dive-bombers continued to harry the enemy retreat to the Don River where a temporary bridge had been constructed near Nakhichevan-on-Don. Dieckmann's vanguard approached the position before Leninawa against heavily defended Soviet positions, although with up to 800m of open territory to his front, German reconnaissance aircraft were called in to provide intelligence on enemy positions. To keep the assault moving, two fast-moving Panzergrenadier companies simply pushed south and secured a bridge some five kilometres west of Rostov-on-Don after first subduing its guards and making them defuse the structure's demolition charges. Swinging around to the north of Leninawa, 13th Panzer Division was similarly halted before the inner defensive line's formidable anti-tank ditch until an engineer platoon from I./66th Panzergrenadier Regiment eliminated the various hazards, including pole-mounted explosives. With support from its 4th Panzer Regiment, the Panzergrenadiers pushed on to the open Stalino–Rostov-on-Don road from the north, where their vehicles mounted a variety of weapons including 75mm short-barrel cannons, 80mm mortars, and the outdated but still useful 37mm anti-tank guns that provided a considerable amount of firepower and mobility.

Mühlenkamp's Panzer battalion made similar progress, and was now fighting through the worker houses and defensive positions in western Rostov-on-Don, and was able to capture its airport. A company from I./Germania arrived to infuse an infantry element to secure any immediate gains, after which armoured elements routed a shaken enemy which surrendered in droves, having abandoned its emplaced artillery intact. After several short but hard engagements against a defence backed by dug-in tanks and anti-aircraft emplacements, the *kampfgruppe* entered Rostov-on-Don proper, gained the Don riverbank to the west of the target bridge, and merged with elements from 13th Panzer Division.

By noon, 57th Panzer Corps forward elements penetrated Rostov-on-Don's innermost defensive positions, with 13th Panzer Division leading Wiking in front, where the latter helped prevent enemy crossings over Don River by sending elements along the north bank to establish blocking positions. With some 50 tanks in its Panzer battalion and an organic Sturmgeschütz battalion, Wiking penetrated Rostov-on-Don's middle defensive line. Having skirted the Don River's generally steep north bank, by 1800 two regiments from 298th Infantry Division had fought through heavy enemy fire in the outer anti-tank ditch and reached Chaltyr, just south of Krym. Between the river channel and the lower south bank, the 2–3km-wide waterway was covered with grass and brush. Germania's *kampfgruppe* had in the meantime moved up to the Mokry Chaltir dry riverbed, where the next morning it was to reconnoitre the Taganrog–Rostov-on-Don road west to the oil pipeline to Armavir.

Bunkers were established throughout Rostov-on-Don to cover important intersections, such as these near administrative buildings on 8 August 1942. These were integrated into other urban defences like sandbag-protected balconies and basement firing positions from which determined NKVD soldiers overwhelmingly fought to the last. (NARA)

With 14th and 22nd Panzer Divisions having pushed into the summer cottages and gardens of Rostov-on-Don's northern edge early on 23 July, 13th Panzer Division and Wiking entered the city's compact and closely built structures, while 125th Infantry Division acted as an immediate reserve. As regular Soviet units filtered rearward, more intent on crossing the Don River than fighting, some 8,700 members of the city's 9th NKVD Motorized Rifle Division fought doggedly to the end. Formed on 1 January 1942, it included 19th and 30th Motorized and 21st and 142nd Rifle regiments, and a field hospital, a formation similar to others from the NKVD that had been created to defend other important cities.

To quickly secure downtown Rostov-on-Don and the main bridge/causeway to Bataisk (a relatively dry region bordered to the east and west by extensive swamps along the Don River), Hauptmann Waldemar von Gazen burst through enemy positions with his 2nd Company, 66th Panzergrenadier Regiment, forcing a crossing over the small Temerink River near where it emptied into the Don River. I./66th Rifle Regiment took the district around the General Post Office and Rostov-on-Don's heavily fortified NKVD headquarters, where the enemy resisted stubbornly and skilfully as fires had steadily broken out across the city, especially among its numerous wooden buildings. Just after dark, units of 22nd Panzer Division accomplished the first link-up between the spearheads of 3rd and 57th Panzer Corps in the centre of the city.

That morning, Wiking made slow progress in street fighting with NKVD forces until 125th Infantry Division moved up in support. Soviet armour relied on infantry perimeters to offer a degree of protection from German anti-tank weapons as bitter house-to-house fighting erupted amid the sweltering 40–45°C temperatures. Having torn up street pavers to create considerable barriers, Soviet engineers and fanatical NKVD fighters also

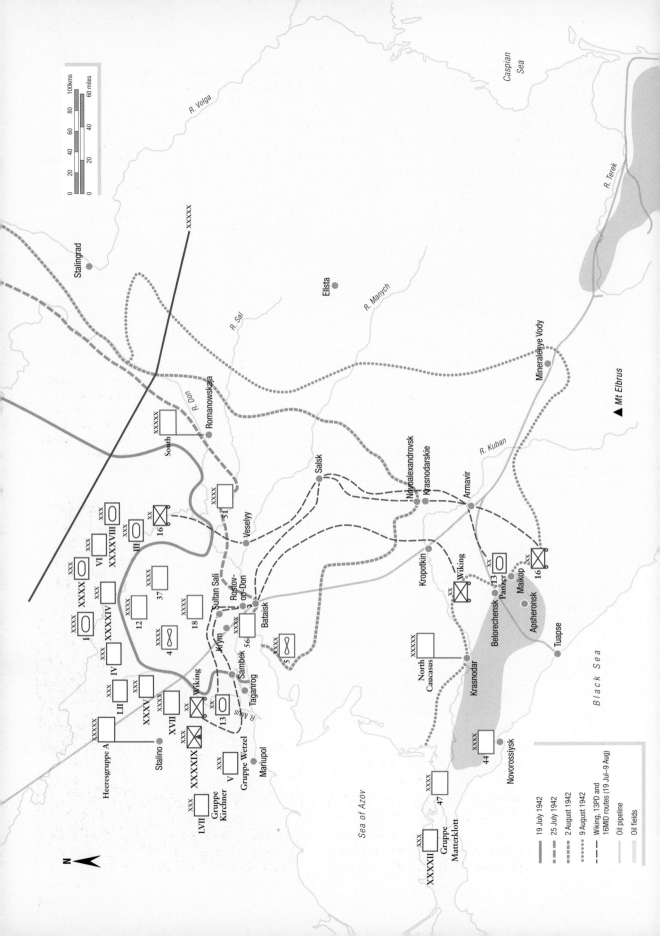

Caspian Sea

R. Volga

R. Terek

Stalingrad

Ellsta

R. Sal

R. Manych

Romanowskaja

R. Don

XXXXX South

Novoalexandrovsk

Krasnodarskie

Salsk

R. Kuban

Armavir

Mineralnye Vody

▲ Mt Elbrus

XXXX 51

Veselyy

Sultan Sali

Rostov-
on-Don

Bataisk

Kropotkin

Wiking

XX 13 Panzer

XXXX 16

XXX VI
XXX XXXVIII

XX 16

XXX III

XXX I
XXX XXXIV

XXXX 37

XXXX 12

XXXX 18

8 4

Krym

56

Belorechensk

Maikop

Apsheronsk

Sambek

Tuapse

5

Taganrog

XXXX IV

XXX LII
XXX XXXV

XVII
Wiking

XX 13

R. Mius

XXXX
XXX North
Caucasus

Krasnodar

Heeresgruppe A

Stalino

XXXXX

XXXXXIX

XXX V
Gruppe Wetzel

Mariupol

Gruppe Kirchner

XXX LVII

XXXX 44

Novorossiysk

XXXX 47

Black Sea

Sea of Azov

XXX XXXXII
Gruppe Matterklott

N

— 19 July 1942
- - - 25 July 1942
····· 2 August 1942
········· 9 August 1942
- - - Wiking, 13PD and
16MID routes (19 Jul–9 Aug)
— Oil pipeline
Oil fields

created large brick strongpoints, steel girders embedded in the ground, and buried mines that hindered enemy attacks. Building entrances were also bricked up or booby-trapped, windows were sandbagged to provide firing positions, balconies had been turned into machine-gun nests, roofs were well-camouflaged hideouts for NKVD snipers, and tens of thousands of Molotov cocktails were created. Soviet troops generally lacked initiative and the ability to adjust to unexpected situations or form even small counter-attacks, although they excelled at taking advantage of defensive positions and terrain features.

Since armoured formations were ill-suited for conducting urban operations due to their limited mobility and the fact that the enemy could target vehicles' weaker plate sections from above, 13th and 22nd Panzer Divisions and Wiking needed help to quickly secure Rostov-on-Don and its Don River crossings for a breakout south. As these formations lacked the necessary infantry numbers to effectively combat stubborn Soviet resistance, particularly its NKVD core, 125th Infantry Division was brought forward to fill the void. Throughout much of the day, Oberst Alfred Reinhardt's Swabians from its 412th Infantry Regiment implemented effective street fighting/assault team tactics in which 1st and 3rd battalions were divided into three assault companies each and supported by a heavy machine gun, anti-tank gun, infantry gun, and a light field howitzer to demolish the barricades, after which 'suspicious points' such as chimneys, basements, and sandbagged balconies were targeted. Backed by 2nd Battalion in reserve, the six company *kampfgruppe* were each assigned defined north–south sectors that were to be thoroughly cleared, while maintaining contact with their neighbours. On reaching each of four successive phase lines, they were to wait for the others to catch up to negate being flanked before repeating the process on Reinhardt's order. As soon as 1st and 3rd battalions secured their sectors, Reinhardt immediately sent in six more assault wedges of 2nd Battalion to double-check their efforts and prevent resistance from rear areas, while all encountered civilians were evacuated from the combat zone to collection points away from the fighting.

German wounded had to be placed in guarded armoured personnel carriers to prevent their being killed by Soviet defenders. Things were worst in the old town and in the harbour district, where the streets, until then more or less straight and regular, degenerated into a maze of crooked lanes. Towed artillery was increasingly a liability in this restricted environment, and *Abzüge* (slang for 'triggers', German machine gunners) were of limited use. Pungent smoke hindered fighting and moving, even though a northerly wind favoured the German

**Opposite:**
As the German summer offensive (Operation *Blau*) cascaded southward from Voronezh, by late July 1942, their effort to secure Rostov, and advance into the North Caucasus commenced. Unwilling to remain static and vulnerable to encirclement, most of the depleted Soviet defenders reached the Western Caucasus Mountains, where they effected a stabilized front line.

The vertical railway lift bridge connecting Rostov and Bataisk on 7 August 1942. Although the original photo caption credited German dive-bombers with destroying the southern span, withdrawing Soviets actually detonated explosives on 23 July. (NARA)

Soldiers from 6th Company, 3rd Railway Engineer Regiment use a temporary footbridge to construct what would be a 296m temporary/war bridge next to the damaged Rostov-on-Don–Bataisk vertical railway bridge. Shown here on 7 August 1942, the 16-support structure was built between 2 August and 1 September. (NARA).

advance as it blew over the Don River. By the time the final 'D' phase line was reached just after dark, only a few hundred metres separated 421st Infantry Regiment from 57th Panzer Corps' forward elements, now occupying positions along the waterway's northern bank. The men were lying among wooden huts, tool-sheds, and heaps of rubble, while machine-gun fire resounded throughout the area and flares lazily drifted to the ground.

During the afternoon, 13th Panzer Division's vanguard, the motorcycle infantry of Oberstleutnant Harald Stolz's 43rd Kradschützen Battalion, had used its recently allocated armoured cars and halftracks to forge a path through central Rostov-on-Don's maze of streets en route to secure the Don railway bridge. Created as a merger between the division's Kradschützen and Panzer Aufklarungs (Reconnaissance) battalions, the 'light' formation respectively provided manoeuvrability and battlefield endurance that helped it weather frequently fierce resistance. As 1st Panzerspähwagen Company reached the river, it found itself too far east of its target. Unable to control the extremely confusing area between the port and the factory facilities, the retreating Soviets blew up one of the railway bridge's spans. While 13th Panzer Division secured the surrounding area, its engineers worked feverishly throughout the night and made the structure serviceable, although initially just for pedestrians and light vehicles. Some 130km upriver, 3rd Panzer Division established a difficult crossing due to the sandy soil and marsh along the south bank near Konstantinovsk, and with support from Oberleutnant Werner John's 3./I Brandenburger Battalion, advanced elements pushed ahead to cross the Ssal River as well.

## Hitler intervenes

Believing that Soviet strength in the southern sector of the Eastern Front was faltering, and looking to quickly complete the final goals of what had to that date been a very successful summer offensive, on 23 July Hitler outlined new goals for *Braunschweig*. With daytime temperatures at his Vinnitsa headquarters as oppressively hot and humid as in the Don River bend, the Führer suffered a severe bout of influenza as he issued Directive 45, in which he ordered Heeresgruppe A to encircle and destroy Timoshenko's remnants that were crossing the Don River and heading into the North Caucasus.

With Hitler personally intervening in what should have been an Army senior command decision, the General Staff was increasingly alarmed by his amateurish, haphazard handling of limited German resources, and the divergent goals that further tasked an already overburdened logistics system and exposed their respective inner flanks to an enemy counter-attack. Heeresgruppe A was to then to secure the Caucasus (Operation *Edelweiss*), while Heeresgruppe B was to capture Stalingrad and, if possible, Astrakhan (Operation *Fischreiher* (Heron)). Considering the former would soon be operating in potentially very rugged terrain, the formation was only allocated three mountain divisions, while the Italian Alpine Corps was redirected to the advance on the Volga River. The Luftwaffe was to continue providing close support to both groups, with General der Flieger (Air General) Karl Pflugbeil's 4th and 8th Air Corps respectively assigned to Heeresgruppe A and B. Attacks were to focus on enemy railways and pipelines, and refineries, storage tanks, and ports used for oil shipments were only to be targeted if conditions on the ground made it absolutely necessary.

German engineers help allied Rumanian Hussars from V Cavalry Corps cross the Kuban River on 16 September 1942 using an eight-man pneumatic 'Grosser Floßsäck 34' assault raft. Having taken Novorossiysk, their front line to the south had stalled at the Western Caucasus Mountains. (NARA)

At dawn on 24 July, Rostov-on-Don's postal district had largely been cleared of Soviet soldiers, but the remaining NKVD defending their headquarters held out until noon, when infantrymen from 13th Panzer Division, with support from 22nd Panzer Division's armour, finally eliminated the last of the city's sizeable centres of resistance. To the west, the former also worked with Wiking to mop up the city centre, while elements from 52th Panzer Corps, 49th Mountain Corps, and 5th Army Corps began to bunch behind them in preparation to cross the Don River and beyond. By 1400 the Germans had cleared the waterway's north bank of enemy soldiers, but new resistance, including several machine-gun nests and infantry guns, was identified on the south side. From here, the swampy terrain around Bataisk could be observed, as could the Soviet retreat across the Don River, often via wooden rafts. Some 15km downriver from the recent German bridgehead at Konstantinovsk, the Soviet 37th Pontoon Bridge Battalion had organized a ferry across the Don River, which continuously transported retreating military and civilian personnel and equipment. Damage from repeated dive-bomber attacks was soon fixed, but when the Germans were able to bring direct ground fire on the crossing, the battalion finally withdrew. Although the weakened Soviet Twelfth and Fifty-First armies continued to resist east of Rostov-on-Don, their position was quickly becoming untenable. To assist in crossing the Ssal and Manych rivers, 2./ and 3./II Brandenburg companies were attached to 40th Panzer Corps, with the former placed in reserve the following day.

## The Brandenburgers seize Bataisk Bridge

With Soviet resistance east of Rostov-on-Don evaporating, during the afternoon the 8./II Brandenburg Battalion of Hauptmann der Reserve Siegfried Grabert was directed through the city to capture the railway bridge/causeway leading to Bataisk and hold them until larger conventional forces arrived. Capitalizing on 1./43rd Kradschützen Battalion's position near the key railway bridge, its 1st Battalion commander was ferried across the Don River alongside 28 volunteers from the battalion's engineer platoon. As the first German unit from Rostov-on-Don to move to the far bank, it quickly established a makeshift command post a few hundred metres west of the structure's southern end. Soon after, Grabert arrived on scene in the area, and he divided his formation into an assault and support force; Leutnant Oskar Hüller soon set off across the 300-metre wide river with his half-company on inflatable assault boats. Once reasonably secure on the south bank, the remainder followed suit, and the entire company assembled at Oberstleutnant Stolz's command post.

After dark, Grabert led half of his command to the causeway, just south of the Don River Bridge, while nearby elements of 43rd Kradschützen Battalion occupied a deep ravine before the enemy-held second bridge, where they provided suppressing fire against Soviets who were now partially surrounded at the main structure some 200 metres to the north. Even though the Soviets employed a heavy machine gun from one of the railway bridge piers, Stolz's men kept the enemy from destroying the structure, and eventually

Ростовъ на/Дону.—Rostofl s/Don. № 4.
Общiй видъ.

Built in 1860 atop Rostov's central embankment, the Cathedral of the Nativity of the Most Holy Mother of God featured a 75m four-level bell tower, snow-white stone walls and gilded domes. Just beyond the North Caucasus Railway depot (lower centre), the Temernik River empties into the Don River (out of view, right). (PD)

eliminated the threat. Hüller led the remainder of 8./ Brandenburger Battalion in support of Grabert as the burning railway bridge and Soviet parachute flares illuminated the advance force struggling southward amid constant artillery and rocket fire. Some 10km to the west, Mühlenkamp conducted a surprise attack that secured a ford that the Soviets were using to cross over the low-lying Don River Delta. As the terrain was too soft for vehicle and heavy weapons, vanguards of 73rd and 298th Infantry Divisions prepared to cross to the south bank before respectively moving eastward toward Bataisk and south-west for Azov. The remainder of both formations continued to push for Rostov-on-Don along the river's northern edge.

An hour after midnight, heavy mortars opened up from the far end of the second bridge, and German crews responded in kind. Soviet tracers set a truck on the structure on fire, which subsequently blew up. At 0230, Grabert gave the signal to attack across the bridge, and the leading squad crept forward across the bridge on both sides of the roadway, followed at short intervals by the other two platoons, but nothing stirred on the Russian side at first. Suddenly alerted, Soviet machine guns and mortars responded, and the German covering party immediately returned what supporting fire they could.

Elements of Grabert's vanguard rushed across the structure, and soon after fired several flares, which indicated to the crew that stayed behind with a heavy machine gun that the crossing had been taken. Their company commander, having suffered a head wound, and with ammunition low, sent a runner back to request support before ordering an attack on the third bridge to commence. From the front, Grabert led his company in another assault amid heavy enemy fire that included machine guns that had been concealed in the marshy islands on either side of the bridge. Several Brandenburgers were hit, including their 'chief', who was struck in the stomach. Responding to calls for immediate help, Dr Helmut Weber and medic Unteroffizier (Corporal) Fohrer swam a small river that passed under the second bridge, as it remained too hazardous to cross, and administered

**24 JULY 1942**

**Grabert's Brandenburgers attack Bataisk Bridge**

morphine to their stricken commander. With so much dependent on quickly securing the roughly 5km-long causeway, 8./Brandenburg Battalion's lead elements overpowered the strong Soviet guard near its southern end. Through the remainder of the night, they remained pinned down before Bataisk, and struggled to retain their gains against enemy counter-attacks.

Only after German tanks arrived at dawn were the Soviets pushed back, while dive-bombers hurried their destruction. Enemy positions in Bataisk were attacked by 40 light and heavy artillery guns, and air strikes were carried out by three dozen Stukas arriving at an opportune time. Then the first reinforcements came up over the causeway and the bridge. Having died near the last pier, Grabert was posthumously awarded the Oak Leaves to his Iron Cross, while some 200m beyond, Hüller's body was found in a swampy hole next to Fohrer's, still clutching his first-aid kit. The tanks subsequently moved over the bridges and headed south. 8./II Brandenburg Battalion achieved its mission, but at a high cost of 17 killed, 16 missing, and 54 wounded. No longer fit for operations, it was withdrawn to regroup. Grabert's operation in Rostov-on-Don was similar to his action during the opening phase of the invasion of Greece the previous year, when his Brandenburger *kampfgruppe* secured a key bridge over the Vardar River against a determined British defence, an action for which he was awarded the first Knight's Cross for a Brandenburger member.

That evening, the elements from 298th and 73rd Infantry Divisions that had set off across the Don River Delta had reached solid terrain to its south, and respectively prepared to advance on Azov and Bataisk. As this area was gradually cleared of Red Army forces, German engineers began repairing the destroyed or damaged bridges along the causeway. Having captured some 83,000 prisoners over the four days it took to capture Rostov-on-Don, Berlin radio announced that 'units of the Army, the Waffen-SS and Slovakian

With the majority of Soviet territory and transportation system undeveloped, a variety of problems could hamper German offensive tempos. Here a pair of connected SdKfz 7 medium halftracks attempts to extricate an 88mm Flak 18 AA/AT gun. (NARA)

troops, supported by the Luftwaffe, have broken through Rostov-on-Don's strongly defended, deeply in place defence positions, along the whole front, and after hard fighting, have taken the important transport and port city.' To facilitate a subsequent, rapid advance into the Caucasus, 5./II Brandenburg Battalion under Hauptmann Johann Zülch was allocated to 13th Panzer Division, with Oberleutnant Karl-Heinz Österwitz's 7./II Battalion in support. Following Grabert's death, Leutnant der Reserve Ernst Prochaska was promoted to interim commander of 8./II Brandenburg Battalion, which was also attached, but had been slated for the Maikop operation, and spent the next several days resting and refurbishing. To Rostov-on-Don's east, 3rd Panzer Division had crossed the Ssal River in force and was pushing south. To address Hitler's fear of the Western Allies opening a 'second front' to relieve pressure on their Soviet ally, he ordered Grossdeutschland to halt before the Manych River for possible redeployment elsewhere, and consequently removed a badly needed armoured unit for use in the Caucasus.

## Beyond the Don River

By 26 July, Bataisk was under German control, with 49th Mountain Corps' infantry formations solidifying positions south of the Don River through which 13th Panzer Division and Wiking would soon attack. Upstream, the Westphalian 16th Infantry (Motorized) Division had already passed through Grossdeutschland's bridgehead, and had pushed between the Soviet Twenty-Fourth and Thirty-Seventh armies to reach the Manych River, with its numerous reservoirs and massive dams that comprised a hydroelectric power system known as Manych-Stroy. In the semi-arid, largely open Kalmyk steppe, hot summer temperatures had dried up many of the region's smaller rivers, although the remaining terrain provided the basis for successive Soviet rearguard positions. In anticipation of defending the Taman Peninsula, the Soviet Adygea and Krasnodar territories incorporated civilian labour to assist the army's construction of defensive lines, and conducted training of combat assault battalions, militia detachments, and volunteer infantry and cavalry. Due to the region's numerous, low-lying salt marshes, fresh-water wells were unavailable.

As 3rd Panzer Division moved to cross the Manych River several kilometres upstream at Proletarskaya, Westphalian 16th Infantry (Motorized) Division's commander, Generalleutnant Sigfrid Henrici, readied to advance across the waterway as well. During final preparations, a German officer landed in a Fieseler 'Storch' and provided aerial photos, which prompted a change of plans. Instead of a bridge, the pictures revealed that one of the two intended crossing sites was actually a long dam that produced a reservoir upstream. The main attack was subsequently changed to a three-pronged operation. Having crossed downstream, 156th Infantry (Motorized) Regiment overcame minor enemy resistance to enter the village of Svoboda, before turning back to move south-east along the waterway. Sixtieth Infantry (Motorized) Regiment attempted to move through Novoselovka further upstream, while in the centre 116th Panzer Battalion, flanked by two companies of 165th Kradschützen Battalion, quickly moved due south to

With Persia a major Lend-Lease route, Red Army formations in the southern areas of the front fielded a large percentage of related vehicles, such as this American M3. Compared to heavier, more robust domestic T-34s, the light foreign model's narrow tracks and inferior armour and armament made them unpopular with Soviet crews. (NARA)

**26 JULY 1942**

**Germans take Bataisk**

secure the heights along the riverbank near Spornyy, where artillery observation positions were soon established. Soon after, a dozen Brandenburgers scouted two suitable crossings near the river's widest part upstream from Spornyy. As preserving the Veselyyskoye Reservoir Dam would enable 3rd Panzer Division to continue its rapid advance south, the village and the blocked and mined structure needed to be taken by surprise.

Between midnight and 0100 on 27 July, German artillery fired on Soviet positions along the river's southern edge. With 39th Panzer Engineer Battalion having brought forward 21 assault boats, an assault company from II./3rd Panzergrenadier Regiment and 3./I Brandenburg Battalion was organized under Oberleutnant der Reserve Walter Tank. With the German bombardment covering the noise of the assault boats' engines, the group reached the far bank without drawing attention. Firing two white Very lights to indicate a successful crossing, the German artillery shifted deeper into the enemy positions, and Tank's men surprised the first two enemy trench lines. Soon, Soviet forces on either flank were alerted, and fired machine guns against follow-on German engineers, which destroyed two boats, but those remaining crossed successfully to deposit what amounted to 120 men, ammunition supplies, and 2nd Battalion headquarters. As dawn approached and enemy fire increased, further ferrying endeavours were halted. Low on ammunition, Luftwaffe fighter-bombers fortuitously arrived to attack the Soviet positions, which allowed a third group to be passed across the river. Tank quickly organized an attack, which took Manych-Story by surprise, as the commander had expected such an action to originate at his front.

At 1000, engineers and 2./165th Kradschützen Battalion under Leutnant Meyer crossed the Novoselovka reservoir in 13 assault boats and established a small bridgehead, while downstream four Panzer IIIs from 3./116th Panzer Battalion and a platoon of mounted engineers rushed the dam, firing as they went. Although a contingent of 3./I Brandenburger Battalion dressed in Soviet uniforms and accompanied by engineers had recently dismantled the detonating mechanism, a Soviet officer had apparently discovered the subterfuge, shot the recently successful enemy crew, and set off the structure's charges. With reservoir water now pouring through the breach, the attack was cancelled and Meyer returned his command to the north bank, as dwindling ammunition meant the position could not be held. In the choppy, 2m-high waves, one of the motor boats stalled, drifted, and upended to drown its occupants. As the area downstream steadily transformed into a 4km-wide lake, the pontoon bridge at Svoboda was swamped, isolating I./156th Motorized Infantry Regiment on the south side, some 15km down river at Malaya Zapadenka. Although the Soviets attempted to capitalize on the situation via a counter-attack, German artillery from the north bank soon broke it up. At 2200 a stable crossing was finally effected at Novoselovka. German engineers would soon construct a bridge over the resulting 92m gap in the dam, although heavier armoured vehicles still needed to be ferried across. As Westphalian 16th Infantry (Motorized) Division disengaged from Heeresgruppe Ruoff to get into the enemy rear areas, its soldiers passed a road sign indicating they were crossing from Europe into Asia.

Early on 27 July, 57th Panzer Corps prepared to move south from Rostov-on-Don, having spent the last two days reorganizing, while 49th Mountain Corps' infantry formations focused on securing crossings over the Kagalnik River, and taking the Kushchevskaya transportation hub nearly 70km south of Bataisk. Against 4th Mountain Division, 73rd Infantry Division on its left flank, and 298th Infantry Division in support, the weakened Soviet Fifty-Sixth Army was forced to continue its retreat, having had to abandon its heavy weapons at the Don River. East of Rostov-on-Don, in response to the Germans having established a front 170km wide and 80km deep, and North Caucasus Front Commander Marshal Semyon Budyonny had few options but to do the same. Against this, six depleted Soviet armies had to cover a 320km front. During the previous month, locals had been organized to create some 2,000km of force-multiplying defensive positions between the Don and Kuban, along the Terek River, on the Taman Peninsula and along the coasts of the Azov and Black Seas, which included 1 million anti-tank and anti-personnel mines, 700 tons of explosives, and 600 tons of barbed wire. Against fast-moving German armoured and mechanized forces, however, such construction remained largely unrealized.

In a report to the Supreme Headquarters, Budyonny wrote about the impossibility of the available forces stopping the enemy advance, and offered to withdraw to at least behind the Kuban and Terek rivers, which would also shorten his logistics from the Black and Caspian Seas, and to defend within the Western Caucasus Mountains; the range's rugged environment, 1,100km length, and 100–200km depth would also negate much of the German

This Type 1 B.1.1 'Distinguished Worker' badge was awarded to NKVD personnel who accomplished important or dangerous assignments. Known as an 'egg' due to its oval shield, it comprised silver and gold plated brass, and a red enamel background scallop encompassed a 42.8mm sword, hammer and sickle, and ribbon inscribed with 'НКВД'. (PD) technical and tactical superiority. Although Stalin had officially blamed the stocky, mustachioed commander for the massive losses around Kiev and Uman the previous year, a situation Stalin had enabled by issuing rigid 'no retreat' orders, Budyonny retained his status, and his prior service in the region during World War I and the Russian Civil War gave him particular insight into the present situation.

## 'Not a single step back!'

On 28 July, German forces around Rostov-on-Don began to push into the Caucasus, while coordinated Luftwaffe support continued to bomb rail and road networks, bridges, and to make regular attacks on the retreating Soviet formations that struggled with limited fuel, ammunition, as well as command and control. Red Army engineers struggled to establish successive rearguard positions to maintain a buffer against the advancing Germans, but with limited time to effect such defences, many of these rearguards became isolated and, forced to rely on their own initiative, many simply dissolved to fight again or defected. That day, the Soviet government announced Rostov-on-Don's fall, which spread additional panic and terror among its soldiers and citizens.

In an effort to counter the growing opinion that the Red Army could remain a viable fighting force by continually withdrawing eastward, Stalin released Order 227, a diatribe stressing that 'these conversations are false and harmful, as they weaken us and strengthen the enemy, for if we do not stop retreating, we will be left without bread, without fuel, without metals, without raw materials, without factories and plants, without railways.' With specific vitriol, he singled out the southern front where 'panic-mongers have abandoned Rostov-on-Don and Novocherkassk without serious resistance and without order from Moscow, thus covering their banners with shame'. As such, Stalin emphasized that 'the conclusion is that it is time to stop the retreat. Not a single step back! This should be our slogan from now.' As a lack of discipline was considered the Red Army's greatest weakness, 'panic-mongers and cowards' were to be executed immediately, and no person or unit was to move without official orders from higher command. In addition to establishing penal battalions and promoting court martials, NKVD 'special detachments' were to ruthlessly enforce the order.

As an expedient to presenting an effective defence, the Supreme Command dissolved General Rodion Malinovsky's shattered South Front, and integrated the remnants into North Caucasus Front under Budyonny. Having previously amalgamated Crimean Front, he now attempted to establish a 200km defensive line along Tikhoretsk–Kropotkin–Novoalexandrovsk–Stavropol, while restoring order and discipline to what had become organized chaos. To improve command and control over 23 infantry divisions, five cavalry divisions and nine infantry brigades, something that was further hampered by several large gaps in his front, the Front Commander divided North Caucasus Front into two entities; Maritime Group headquartered at Krasnodar (Eighteenth, Fifty-Sixth, and Forty-Seventh armies) and Don Group, which operated to the east at Stavropol (Fifty-First, Thirty-Seventh, and Twelfth armies). Comprised of divisions fielding as few as 500 personnel, some staff, and miscellaneous units, the Soviet strength in the Caucasus lacked the numbers and organization to form a continuous front line, let alone offer anything beyond limited, temporary resistance. Beating the Germans to the Western Caucasus Mountain foothills seemed the only option to remain viable.

The Führer's Directive of 31 July demanded that on the Caucasus front the second phase of *Edelweiss* was now to begin: the capture of the Black Sea coast. Heeresgruppe A was to employ its fast formations, now grouped under the command of First Panzer Army, in the direction of Armavir and Maikop. Heeresgruppe Ruoff, with Kirchner's 57th Panzer Corps, were to drive for Novorossiysk and Tuapse along the Sea of Azov coast to Batumi. The German and Rumanian mountain divisions of 49th Mountain Corps were to be employed on the left wing across the high Caucasian passes to outflank Tuapse and Sukhumi. Hitler's decision to push ahead simultaneously with the operations against the Caucasus and against Stalingrad meant that supplies also had to be divided. And since greater distances had to be tackled in the south, the Quartermaster-General of the Army General Staff had given the Caucasus front priority in fuel-supplies, and many motorized long-distance supply columns originally destined for Sixth Army were redirected to the south.

With severe fuel shortages and stiff enemy resistance between the Don and Volga Rivers hampering Sixth Army's push on Stalingrad, Hitler once again incorporated a change into an active operation, by redirecting Fourth Panzer Army (minus 40th Panzer Corps) from the Caucasus front and sending it to assist Heeresgruppe B. Generalfeldmarschall Wilhelm List had never desired the formation, as it accomplished little more than clogging his already overburdened road network. As a result of undertaking this movement now, it unnecessarily complicated logistics, weakened List's offensive striking power in the Caucasus, and arrived too late to help capture Stalingrad. By abandoning a single, defined centre of gravity, the German High Command had manoeuvred itself into an increasingly difficult position, which if not corrected would relinquish operational control to its enemy in the southern theatre.

The imposing terrain near Pshekha-Su, roughly 60km south of Maikop and at the western edge of the Caucasus Mountains, is representative of the range, and illustrates the importance of securing passes. (Lyubov Glazkova)

## The Brandenburgers' chance to infiltrate Maikop

On 1 August, Heeresgruppe Ruoff and First Panzer Army continued to push into the North Caucasus, the Soviet Union's most fertile and productive grain area, with its seemingly unending corn and sunflower fields. Having made the furthest German penetration in the south to date, a *kampfgruppe* from 13th Panzer Division advanced into the Kuban River Valley and

# THE ADVANCE ON MAIKOP

## JULY–AUGUST 1942

As the German 13th Panzer Division, and Wiking, respectively advanced on
Maikop and Belorechensk, enroute toward Tuapse, Brandenburger forces
attempted to secure the area's oil facilities and bridges over the Belaya River.

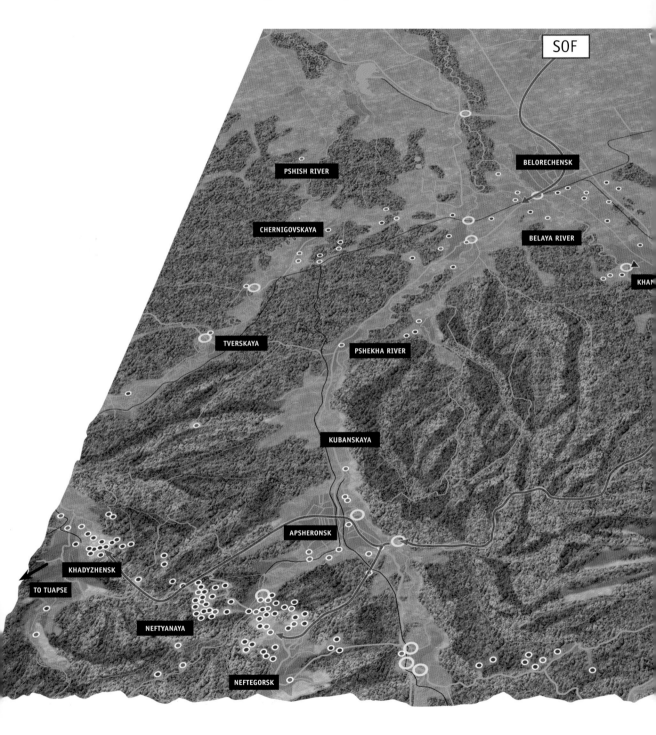

SOF

PSHISH RIVER

BELORECHENSK

CHERNIGOVSKAYA

BELAYA RIVER

KHAN

TVERSKAYA

PSHEKHA RIVER

KUBANSKAYA

APSHERONSK

KHADYZHENSK

TO TUAPSE

NEFTYANAYA

NEFTEGORSK

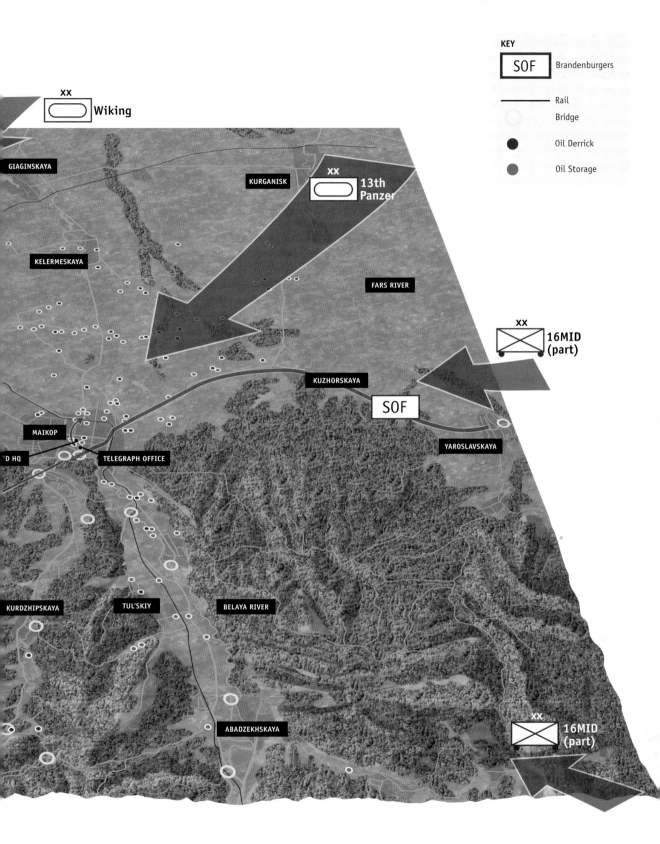

KEY

SOF    Brandenburgers

——    Rail

◯    Bridge

●    Oil Derrick

●    Oil Storage

XX
Wiking

GIAGINSKAYA

KURGANISK

XX
13th
Panzer

KELERMESKAYA

FARS RIVER

XX
16MID
(part)

KUZHORSKAYA

SOF

MAIKOP

D HQ

TELEGRAPH OFFICE

YAROSLAVSKAYA

KURDZHIPSKAYA

TUL'SKIY

BELAYA RIVER

XX
16MID
(part)

ABADZEKHSKAYA

captured Novoalexandrovsk later in the day, some 30km ahead of its parent unit, and 65km north of the important road hub at Armavir. Beyond that, 100km to the south-west lay Maikop and the oil fields around Neftegorsk. Although the German pace remained rapid, it would still take several days to secure the latter, during which time the Soviets would likely destroy the area's numerous derricks and related equipment rather than abandon them intact. Much as they had done with bridges, the Brandenburgers were tasked with infiltrating enemy lines to Maikop, where they were to ease the way for the anticipated arrival of 13th Panzer Division, as well as securing the area's oil assets until conventional forces arrived. With a recently returned German patrol having described some 700–800 enemy soldiers encamped in a village just to the south that had been cut off in the general Soviet retreat, Fölkersam's opportunity had arrived.

## Behind Soviet lines

Anticipating the fear their presence would instill, Fölkersam waited until after dark to lead his 62-man 'NKVD' contingent through friendly lines around Novoalexandrovsk and into enemy territory. Considering the mission's context and duration, in which Soviet security would be alert to infiltration and any detail out of the ordinary would draw attention, it would have been unnecessarily risky to wear German uniforms under their NKVD ones. As doctrine dictated when operating behind enemy lines, each soldier carried a cyanide capsule in case they should be captured, as torture and death would likely follow. With the moon only just starting to wane, a degree of natural light was available, as the men walked due south along a farm path surrounded by broad fields of sunflowers and scrub foliage. The rapid German advance had translated into a porous front line, and although the threat of landmines or established defenses was minimized, remaining unobserved would have been paramount to have best enabled the Brandenburgers not accidentally to draw friendly or enemy fire, and to make contact at their choosing.

Over the previous two days, the Soviet Ninth Army had been withdrawing through the area ahead of the German advance, and 1st Separate Cavalry Corps had moved up to establish defensive positions along the rail line and Rasshevatka River that ran through Novoalexandrovsk along a roughly east–west line. As the cavalry formation's second incarnation (the first having been destroyed during *Barbarossa's* initial stage), it had served under Budyonny's direct authority since 20 May 1942, and had recently fought in Rostov-on-Don's defence. With German forces seemingly unstoppable, and now roughly halfway between the Don River and the Caucasus Mountain foothills, the corps commander, Major General Vasily Kotelnikov, could hardly have looked forward to engaging 3rd Panzer Division with his three rifle brigades and a single rifle division possessing just 500 rifles for its 3,000 soldiers.

At dawn on 2 August the Brandenburgers approached the village of Krasnodarskie, where in addition to numerous horses and camels, vehicles and fuel were also nearby. Seeing an opportunity, Fölkersam quietly had his men surround their sleeping enemy before having them suddenly fire their weapons into the air. The startled mix of Muslim Kuban Cossacks, Kyrgyzs, Circassians and Turkomans, as well as Ukrainians, Georgians, Russians, and even Siberians, sprang to life. Before they could gather their wits, the 'NKVD' contingent disarmed and herded them into the village centre along the main road.

Historically, the populations of the Ukraine and North Caucasus were anti-Soviet, and as the Brandenburgers asserted their 'authority' it became evident that none but the minority Russians and Serbians wanted to rejoin their units; the remainder desired nothing more than exiting the combat zone and deserting. For dramatic effect, Fölkersam stood on one of the trucks' hoods, as some of his men gathered around him for security. Improvising a speech, the 'NKVD' commander sarcastically demanded to know what was happening, and if they had thoughts of deserting. Apparently they did not understand that Stalin had anticipated the current situation, and had set a trap in which the Caucasus Mountains would be the Fascists' grave. A few Cossacks made sarcastic remarks, and when one of their ranks laughed, Fölkersam motioned to his men, and two 'NKVD' soldiers manhandled the offender from the group and asked if they should shoot him. Fölkersam brushed it off with 'later', and returned to his speech, which emphasized that although they deserved to die, he was aware of 'filthy snakes' in the group that had acted as ringleaders, and that he should be thanked for preventing their committing treason. As an example to those gathered, Fölkersam ordered the Cossacks separated, and along with 30 of his men, mounted a truck and two cars, and herded the condemned group away to the north.

After some 45 minutes, Fölkersam halted the group at a ravine, exited his car, and asked the group's *ataman* (leader) to confirm that his followers wanted to go over to the Germans, as other Cossacks had done over the preceding weeks, with many then transitioning to fight the Soviets. As the Cossack leader was naturally confused and suspicious, the 'NKVD' major elaborated that his command would soon shoot into the air to make the soldiers in the village believe the group had been liquidated, after which the 'condemned' were to remain hidden for at least an hour before mixing with the confusion of refugees and Red Army rearguards, and making for German lines. The *ataman* agreed, and after conducting their mock execution, Fölkersam's detachment returned to the village, where those gathered had heard the shooting. He told the Russian and Siberian officers that they should make for the Soviet lines, and that he would deal with the Ukrainians and Caucasians as he had with the Cossacks. The Russians and Siberians soon mounted trucks and headed south, while the Brandenburgers waited in the village a requisite amount of time before releasing the remaining enemy soldiers as with the previous group. Having commandeered vehicles, Fölkersam's command set off southward where they joined the ragged migration of vehicles, soldiers, and civilians. In addition to the high daytime temperatures, sporadic thunderstorms, and considerable dust clouds, the volume of traffic greatly delayed the Brandenburgers' progress, and the 55km drive to Armavir took the entire day. After passing through Grigoripolnaskaja, they took the main road to Armavir, which ran parallel with the Kuban River before crossing over the waterway's east side at Prochnookopskaya.

At the end of the 19th century, Maikop consisted of little more than a scattering of single-storey structures, a bridge over the Belaya (White) River leading to Tuapse, and the Assumption Cathedral. (N. Burhaylo)

After a taxing drive, the Brandenburger vehicles entered Armavir early on Monday, 3 August. As they approached the Armavir–Tuapse Railway, which comprised several parallel tracks at the city's main train station, they were stopped by actual NKVD personnel attempting to regulate military vehicles through the overwhelming chaos. Fölkersam exited his car and walked up to report to the dour colonel in charge. When asked who he was, the Brandenburger commander responded that he was a 'Major Truchin' from 124th NKVD Rifle Brigade on special assignment (under Colonel Sergei Gorokhov) from Aleksei Zhadov, commander of Sixty-Sixth Army at Stalingrad. Although the colonel knew nothing of the unit or assignment, he smiled as if having been previously been made aware of Truchin's arrival, and expressed that his command had been expected the day before. The colonel also explained that he was directing armoured and cavalry forces towards Maikop and Tuapse, and that as Soviet infantry was also gathering in these areas, Truchin needed to be vigilant as spies were known to have infiltrated the latter. With no reason to further detain the Brandenburgers, the checkpoint commander moved them through.

As First Panzer Army advanced south through the Caucasus and attempted to maintain contact with Seventeenth Army, it was unable to allocate sufficient resources to eliminate Soviet formations falling back on Grozny and the Caspian Sea, a situation for which List could now have used Fourth Panzer Army. To the east, the Soviets had largely vacated the generally desolate landscape as it served little purpose to defend it. The native Muslim population was overwhelmingly friendly, believing the advancing Germans brought liberation and independence from Soviet rule (and before that Russian oppression). Whole tribes and villages volunteered to fight the Red Army, against German High Command's wishes, with many hoisting the crescent flag of Islam in celebration over their dwellings.

## Guests of the NKVD

After a hot, dusty drive amid the throngs of men and materiel moving southward, on reaching Maikop Fölkersam's group drove directly to the city's NKVD headquarters, a three-storey building a few blocks north of the Belaya River. As Fölkersam ascended the front stairs where a few officers had gathered, one who happened to have been with the Russians at Novoalexandrovsk approached to say that he had already made a report of Truchin's liquidation of the Cossacks, and that his arrival in the city was expected. As Fölkersam entered the building, the NKVD commander, General Perscholl, enthusiastically received him. As the 'NKVD' major moved to offer his command and special orders papers, the general gestured to put them away, but Fölkersam presented them anyway. The general expressed his agreement that the Cossacks had always been traitors, and that Fölkersam's actions would serve as an example to others of a similar mind. Shaking hands and inviting the major's command to be his guests, Perscholl ordered that a large villa and garage next door be confiscated for their use. Considering the virtual absence of living space in a city packed with refugees, the comfortable accommodation and relative privacy was certainly welcome. With six or seven days before the expected arrival of friendly forces, the Brandenburgers were relatively free to prepare for their upcoming mission in private. Although a careful examination of the room did not uncover hidden microphones, caution dictated that any discussion about their mission was conducted with a radio on to mask their voices. After getting settled in, Fölkersam and the general spent the evening drinking and talking.

With German forces continuing to advance toward Maikop, on 4 August Wiking was to remain close to the retreating Soviets to best secure the Goythsky Pass through the rugged Western Caucasus before pushing for Tuapse along the only road route. Mountain units were to be brought forward as soon as possible to secure additional routes, which were commonly little more than mule paths. To the Germans, these comprised roads designated as 1 (Novorossiysk–Batumi), 2 (Maikop–Tuapse), 3 (Maikop–Samur–Lasarevskoye), and 4 (Maikop–Dahovskaya–Guzeripl–Krasnaya–Polyana–Adler).

On 5 August, Fölkersam's men went about their 'NKVD' duties, while quietly scouting their mission area, but he noticed that over the previous two days some seemed to be taking their roles less seriously than was required to avoid unwanted scrutiny, especially at a time of hypervigilance in uncovering spies. In response, he strongly reiterated the mission's seriousness, and stressed not to forget their training at the special school at Olsztyn. 'Comrade Wuischkin' was singled out for being too gentle in performing his role, and that he needed to act like more like an NKVD member. 'Comrade Lebedev' was told that his job didn't entail chasing after girls at the nearby Univermag department store, while 'Comrade Balamontow' lacked the appropriate sneer or attitude when using the word 'Fascist'. Told to equate its use with derisive words and to maintain a suspicious gaze when expressing it, the Brandenburger explained sheepishly that he had simply been unfamiliar with the word. Two members, Fähnrich (Army Officer Candidate/Cadet Sergeant) Franz Koudele ('Lieutenant Protoff'), and Feldwebel (Staff Sergeant) Landowsky ('Lieutenant Oktschakow'), however, had played their parts well. In discussing tasks, some groups had to first scout the location of oil depots and fields, and then develop a plan on how to prevent their destruction. Fölkersam desired to go to the front to reduce the number of casualties among the advancing Germans, who were expected to arrive on 8 August at the earliest.

**2 AUGUST 1942**

**Fölkersam's Brandenburgers penetrate Soviet lines**

## Touring the Maikop defences

Having spent a second night drinking with General Perscholl, Fölkersam was now on excellent terms with his 'superior', who invited him on a tour of Maikop's defences. With the southern half of the city resting in an enclave where the Belaya River ran along the terrain in which the heavily wooded, Caucasus Mountain foothills met the relatively flat country to the north, the anticipated German attack would undoubtedly strike into the latter. As such, the general had arrayed all of his artillery in three staggered lines around the intersection of the main road north and the railway that ran from Belorechensk and terminated a few kilometres to the south-east at Kamersomostakaja, with each line reinforced by anti-tank emplacements. Asked for his opinion, Fölkersam responded that they were excellent, provided the Fascist tanks remained on the road and moved in a row. Should they instead spread out in a line across the sunflower fields, or from an unexpected direction, a more distributed force distribution was needed. Fölkersam added that such a scenario had been the Soviet defenders' undoing at Taganrog and Rostov-on-Don, as German spearheads simply skirted the main road and attacked from unexpected directions. For emphasis, he pointed out potential locations from which an attack could originate, and that to prevent the enemy from penetrating into the south of the city, a staggered defence was always preferable. The general agreed, and expressed satisfaction that with the 'major's' concurrence, it would be easier to get the positions rearranged. Subsequently tasked to begin rearrangements that night, one key aspect of Fölkersam's mission had been addressed.

## The Panzers approach

On 3 August 1942, 13th Panzer and 16th Motorized Infantry Divisions crossed the Kuban River at Armavir en route to Maikop, with Wiking covering their right. (Vladimir Volkov)

As 13th Panzer Division established a foothold north of Armavir and used a pontoon bridge to cross the Kuban River and enter the town, the troops seized numerous weapons and equipment, including 50 aircraft. German forces had been sent along the Armavir–Kropotkin Railway, which the Luftwaffe and Wiking artillery had bombed in an effort to prevent the many trains loaded with war materiel from escaping southward. Having failed to

encircle North Caucasus Front between the Don and Kuban rivers, List changed the direction of his main attack. First Panzer Army was to turn to the south-west of Maikop and Armavir, while Seventeenth Army continued for Krasnodar. Having taken Armavir, First Panzer Army commander Generaloberst Edwald von Kleist had Wiking and 13th Panzer Division cross the Kuban River and push into a gap between the Soviet Twelfth and Thirty-Seventh armies, which conducted determined but uncoordinated stands that soon dissolved or were overrun. Within a day, TBM personnel had moved forward to establish its base camp in the city.

That night, the Stavka ordered Budyonny to cover the important Maikop–Tuapse axis, but with little time to prepare an effective defence it was a difficult task, as each division now covered an average of 40km of front. Included in this response, Eighteenth Army covered Maikop, with its 17th Cavalry Corps, as well as 383rd 'Miners' and 236th Rifle divisions, positioned around Belorechensk, where the latter two units' lack of organic transport hindered their battlefield capabilities. Extending south-east to Maikop and beyond included the above corps' 13th (Cossack) Cavalry Division and 30th and 31st Rifle Divisions, respectively south-west and just north of Maikop, and 9th Motorized Division east of the city. With negligible coordination among the defending formations and a lack of ammunition, food, and weapons, many overwhelmed Soviet defenders continued to move for the forested foothills to their rear. As the Germans moved towards Maikop and Khadyzhensk, only 31st Rifle and 9th Motorized Rifle divisions offered resistance while nearby units struggled rearward, including 17th Cavalry Corps, which pulled back to cover the Belaya River. As the German front approached Maikop, every resident had been tasked with around-the-clock construction of fortifications along the approaches to the city.

By the evening of 7 August, 13th Panzer Division had advanced to just north of Maikop, while to the north-west, Wiking made similar progress at Belorechensk. In the former city, chaos reigned and looting was rampant as soldiers and civilians attempted to extricate themselves from the area. Having gathered the remaining information they believed necessary to undertake their mission's final stage earlier the previous day, and finding Perscholl absent from his headquarters and the archives removed, Fölkersam exploited the situation and enacted the agreed-upon plan involving three groups. The largest, under Sergeant Landowski, was to head to the south-west to prevent, as much as possible, the destruction of the oil facilities, and abort demolition of the wells by eliminating the real demolition parties, then pretending to undertake such actions themselves. Koudele-Protoff led the second, which was to remain in Maikop to sever telephone and telegraph contact with the city. Fölkersam had originally wanted to lead the first group, but that night he learned that two Soviet brigades had moved up from the south-east and had occupied defensive positions along the city's north-eastern edge, along the expected path of 13th Panzer Division. Hoping to prevent the new arrivals from negating his success in diminishing Maikop's defenses, he instead led the third group to ensure oncoming German conventional forces encountered as little opposition as possible.

**7 AUGUST 1942**

**13th Panzer Division approaches Maikop**

# THE BRANDENBURGERS' 'NKVD' UNIFORMS

On 10 July 1937, the Soviet M37 (1937) uniform (peaked cap, gymnastiorka service pull-over, and breeches) officially superseded the M35 for all NKVD state security, interior, and border personnel, and incorporated standardized rank insignia as with the RKKA. Interior troops, such as this sergeant (**1**) and major (**2**), were increasingly allocated to frontline duties in 1941/42, in addition to those of police.

Also shown are a German 3kg Geballte Ladung (concentrated charge) (**3**) and a backpack (**4**) that could hold two Nebelkerzen 39 smoke grenades (**5**) and a 3kg explosive charge.

## The Brandenburgers strike

Early on 9 August, Fölkersam received a radio message that patrols from 13th Panzer Division were just 20km away, and his men set off in four cars, some armed and standing on the running boards, and negotiated the unimpeded flood of refugees heading south. Once at Maikop's northern edge, the Brandenburgers parked the cars near an isolated building where the army's message switching centre was located. Nearby, German 150mm rounds landed along the now empty road that ran north out of the city, occasionally hitting their Soviet targets. Six Brandenburgers crept forward to place explosive packs at the communication centre, and when they returned, the group quickly ran the gauntlet of friendly artillery fire. A few minutes later, a powerful explosion destroyed the switching centre building, but amid the deluge of German artillery rounds the incident garnered little attention.

Fölkersam then went to the Soviet artillery officer, a lieutenant colonel he had previously met during his first inspection of Maikop's defences with the general, and asked for a situation report. The artillery officer responded that the Germans were attacking from the north, to which Fölkersam provided misinformation that the enemy's main effort was actually attacking from a different direction, and that the front had already pushed south of Maikop. After a failed attempt to establish outside contact, due to the recently destroyed facility, the lieutenant colonel quickly ordered a ceasefire, and prepared his command to withdraw. Asked to join him, Fölkersam responded that his 'NKVD' command would do its duty and remain behind as a sacrificial blocking force.

Fölkersam then took his team to the positions occupied by one of the newly arrived brigades and introduced himself to the commanding general, and advised that the position was almost cut off. A stickler for proper procedures, the senior officer seemingly had little respect for the NKVD, and

As one of Germany's earliest air defence vehicles, the SdKfz 10/4, featured folding crew seats and sides to provide its 20mm Flak 30/38 L/112.5 gun with an excellent field of fire. Seen here in the Caucasus on 12 November 1942, each tows an SdAh 51 trailer that contains ammunition, gunsights, and a rangefinder. (NARA)

on being made aware of the crippled phone lines and the declining artillery support, eyed the newcomers with suspicion and began to ask uncomfortable questions. With the tension between the two mounting, a winded liaison officer rushed into the command post to report the withdrawal of the artillery. Apparently satisfied with Fölkersam's insight, the general subsequently ordered a retreat as well. Adjacent units noticed their withdrawing comrades and quickly followed suit.

In the meantime, Koudele and his command entered the North Caucasus message centre within Maikop. They acted as if they had authority over those in the building and spoke loudly about their having to evacuate, when the actual commander, a major, approached to say that just because the NKVD had left the city, he didn't need to do the same. Feigning offence, Koudele retorted that he was a lieutenant of the NKVD and that he needed to take back his comment, to which the now sheepish major stated that he had not received such corroborating orders. He added that a new front line was forming near Apschetousk, and knowing that the communications were severed, prodded the stubborn officer to call the Central Office to verify the situation. Koudele stressed that he had orders to blow the building up, and that if the major and his men remained at their post, in 15 minutes they would all be blasted into the air and the lines to North Caucasus Central would cease to exist. Finally relenting, the commander and his subordinates quickly departed.

The Brandenburgers now set about manning the radio and telephone positions, responding to all queries to the effect that communications were increasingly impossible as the Germans had pushed beyond the city, and that a general evacuation order toward Tuapse had been issued. As many Soviet commanders did not wish to be left behind, increasing numbers of Soviet defenders disengaged from the fight and withdrew. With 13th Panzer Division's spearheads pushing into the city's northern edge around noon, Koudele and his men finally ceased their ruse, which, with incoming encrypted messages demanding to know their identity, had outlived its usefulness. As a final productive action, the Brandenburgers destroyed the facility using grenades.

Having the largest command, Landowski tried to use a field telephone that was connected with the main telephone cable to contact an army authority who could order those elements manning the region's oil facilities to stand down, but neither it nor a wireless option were answered. Forced to undertake this operation on their own, he divided his command into smaller 'NKVD' groups to best cover the wide Neftegorsk–Maikop area. Having planned for such a contingency, Landowski's men arrived at a run, and told those on duty that orders 'from above' had authorized the 'NKVD' men with taking over the tasks of the police station and destroying the facilities in anticipation of the German arrival. Considering such a wide area needed to be covered, not every Brandenburger team was able to convince the real guards to withdraw. With the Soviet head of security in the area suspicious of such activities, and unable to contact an official higher authority, he ordered all oil derricks and storage tanks destroyed. As initial explosions alerted other nearby areas, they followed suit. The losses marred

**Overleaf**:

With the German 13th Panzer Division's assault on Maikop imminent, during the night of 8/9 August, Ensign Francis Koudele led Brandenburgers in NKVD uniforms to the city's telegraph office. After convincing the Soviet facility commander to join the 'ordered' retreat south, the Germans proceeded to operate the switchboards, telling all callers that Maikop was to be evacuated, before destroying the building's equipment and disappearing.

Epitomizing the German effort to secure Soviet oil production facilities in the Caucasus, a rig at Neftegorsk lies in ruins on 16 October 1942. (NARA)

an otherwise flawless operation for the Brandenburgers. However, of Maikop's roughly 30 oil storage tanks and 15 derricks, the Brandenburgers managed to save all but one of the former.

For the remainder of the day, fierce but isolated fighting continued in and around Maikop and north-west to Khan. To its immediate east, cadets from the Orlovsky Tank School provided a 'Maikopskaya Tank Brigade', and established three hastily prepared defensive lines in which they manoeuvred some of their T-34 medium tanks into camouflaged, hull-down positions. When the Germans attempted to overrun the area using two attacking prongs backed by artillery, the Soviet commander, Lieutenant Proskurin, initiated an ambush astride the main road that temporarily rebuffed them, with the loss of nine armoured vehicles including seven tanks. A follow-up German attack achieved similar but less damaging results. To help get the German advance moving, they called in a twin-engine Focke-Wulf Fw 189 reconnaissance plane, which provided an alternate attack route that eventually bypassed the troublesome position. On the evening of 9 August, 13th Panzer Division stormed Maikop, taking around a thousand prisoners and capturing 50 undamaged aircraft at the airfield just north-west of the city.

## Belaya Bridge

Having received orders to take the road bridge at Belaya River on 10 August, Prochaska led a 24-man team from his 8./II Battalion in front of a I./66th Panzergrenadier Regiment *kampfgruppe* at 1300 to assist its crossing. Dressed in Red Army uniforms, the Brandenburgers rode in four captured trucks, where after crossing the Giaga River some 20km from their destination they sped toward the north side of the largely abandoned city of Belorechensk as if just ahead of German spearheads. Once in the urban environment, the trucks slowed their pace as they merged with throngs of retreating enemy soldiers and civilians at around 1700. As they approached the bridge over the Belaya River, they were stopped by a Soviet general and asked their business, to which Prochaska reported that his command was to assist with protecting the crossing. Apparently satisfied, the general motioned the group to their stated task.

On approaching the bridge, which was rigged with demolition charges and guarded by a platoon-sized unit, the Soviet policeman directing traffic stepped forward to stop the lead vehicle to permit the dense foot traffic to thin. After a few moments, permission was given to cross, but with the truck's starter failing to turn over, the helpful enemy soldier helped crank it back to operation. On crossing to the Belaya's southern shore, Prochaska ordered his men to dismount, armed with PPSh-41 machine pistols. The Brandenburgers shot the crew of a nearby tanker truck, then quickly cut the main detonation wire and removed the explosives from the bridge piers. He then fired two white flares to indicate success, to which a Nordland Panzer battalion that had just arrived at Belorechensk responded. Cries of enemy 'tanks' reverberated through the panicked crowd as they converged on the road and the adjacent rail bridge. A Panzer IV overcame the obstacles and crossed the bridge. Infantrymen and anti-tank guns soon followed. Prochaska was shot (likely by a sniper) and died while running back across the bridge. Leutnant Zülch was killed by a high-explosive round near the baggage train. Feldwebel Schink, Gefreiter Walter Perunter, and three other Brandenburgers were also killed.

Earlier in the afternoon, the Red Army defenders at Abadzekh gathered what weapons and vehicles they could and suddenly withdrew into the dark woods to their south. As per that day's Directive of the Supreme Command (170564), North Caucasus Front commander stated that in the present situation 'the most fundamental and dangerous [threat] to his formation

Bridge over the Belaya River at Belorechensk. On 10 August, a team from 8./II Brandenburger Battalion dressed in Soviet uniforms secured the structure, removed its explosive charges, and facilitated Wiking's southward advance. (Lyubov Glazkova)

More of the destroyed oil equipment with which 3rd Technical Mineralöl Brigade personnel had to contend on 16 October 1942 near Neftegorsk. (NARA)

and the Black Sea coast is [the German] movement in the direction from Maikop to Tuapse.' Eighteenth Army and 17th Cavalry Corps stood in the German path.

Despite fierce resistance at Krasnodar some 80km to the west, the German 5th Army Corps took the city, while Third Rumanian Army advanced in a south-westerly direction toward the lower Kuban River. Fifty-Seventh Panzer Corps, which had been slowed down by the many destroyed ridges, penetrated into Maikop and the surrounding area. Soon after, the Germans captured valuable staff documents of the Soviet troops, including updated Western Caucasus topographical maps and the Red Army's defensive positions and communications network. Able to revise their older, often incomplete maps, the Germans also uncovered intelligence on Turkey and that border's fortified areas. Thick smoke plumes to the south indicated that the Soviets had set fire to many of the area's oil facilities. The Soviets had started the dismantling of Krasnodar's oil facilities in November 1941, but when it was realized the Germans would be held before Rostov-on-Don, within a month they had conducted repairs, often with US equipment.

With these assets now directly threatened, the Soviets destroyed many of the area's 755 oil wells, 11 compressor installations, and a pipeline. Soon after these areas were secured by conventional forces, elements from TBM moved in to address the oil situation. Although German fuel shortages had dogged their advance through the North Caucasus, the situation had steadily worsened, and sending 9th Panzer Corps south-east in order to pursue the retreating enemy (who did not even destroy the bridges any more) could not be done effectively. Fuel was distributed to vanguards, but at the expense of other units, and pursuits were frequently stopped by only minor resistance.

**10 AUGUST 1942**

**Prochaska's Brandenburgers take the Belaya Bridge**

# AFTERMATH

Around Maikop, scattered and retreating Soviet groups engaged in short battles with advancing German ground and air elements, as both groups negotiated the throngs of refugees. Contrary to Soviet expectations, First Panzer Army deviated from its southern axis of advance, turning east to skirt the Western Caucasus foothills and push for Grozny and Vladikavkaz. Although the Germans had captured Maikop – something trumpeted on the radio, and for which 13th Panzer Division's commander was awarded the Oak Leaves to the Knight's Cross – Soviet resistance was stiffening throughout the mountainous south. On 11 August, Heeresgruppe B issued a directive for the continuation of the operation, in which Seventeenth Army was to focus its efforts south of the Western Caucasus Mountains, while First Panzer Army would operate to the north of the mountain range. Third Rumanian Army, which remained attached to Heeresgruppe Ruoff, was to penetrate the Taman Peninsula from the rear to facilitate additional forces in crossing from the Crimea. When List issued the order, he understood that the objectives were likely unattainable given his limited, increasingly dispersed forces and the supply difficulties, although the enemy's continued avoidance of a sustained stand-up fight left room for optimism.

Throughout the remainder of August, German forces continued to make progress, albeit at a noticeably slower pace, as they moved into the Western Caucasus Mountains and attempted to secure crossings, specifically along the road to Tuapse on the Black

By 15 August 1942, the exhausting German offensive tempo into the Caucasus necessitated rest whenever possible. This army soldier (as evidenced by the licence plate's 'WH') operated in a three-man reconnaissance team that would fight dismounted. Note the MP-40 and censored plate numbers and sidecar insignia on the Triumph 250 BD W motorcycle–sidecar. (NARA)

Sea coast. The Front Military Council ruled that Soviet failures along the Belaya River between Belorechensk and Maikop and later at Khadyzhensk were 'solely the fault of the commander of XVII Cavalry Corps, Major General Kirichenko, and Regimental Commissar Ochkina', stating that between 12 and 16 August they failed to provide sufficient initiative and continually repositioned the corps headquarters to keep it as far as 50km from the front line, which hampered command and control. The formation therefore looked to redeem itself in combat by making an equally determined effort to defend its blocking position. The considerable force-modifying terrain also enabled limited numbers of Red Army defenders to hold off much larger forces, and permitted Transcaucasian Front to bring up reinforcements. Although the Red Army generally lacked experience in conducting mountain operations, had minimal communication with formation staffs, and lacked maps, its troops used mines, rubble, and dug-in machine gun positions to good effect in the restricted, forested environment. Such efforts permitted effective stands to the east as well, especially along the Terek and Baksan Rivers, and the mountain passes leading to key locations including Grozny, Baku, Ordzhonikidze, and Tbilisi.

With the German successes in the Caucasus a concern to not just the Soviets, but also to the Western Allies, the British repeatedly expressed concerns that the situation posed a direct threat to the Allies' interests in India and its supply routes through Persia. Receiving vague assurances, the British pressed the matter and offered to provide their air field units and similar support to the region. Although Stalin accepted a considerable amount of Allied-supplied armaments, in accordance with an American and British plan code-named 'Velvet' that was developed over the summer, 20 American and British air squadrons were to ensure the defence of the Caucasus and Caspian, and even a redeployment of the latter's Tenth Army in the Caucasus was planned. Suspicious and distrustful of such direct foreign assistance, Stalin rebuffed the idea, stating 'there is no war in the Caucasus; the war is in Ukraine.' He elaborated that 25 divisions would be drafted to defend the mountain positions and passes and that they would hold key areas such as Batumi and Baku until winter stymied further German efforts in the region. Stalling for time, Stalin confided in the British Prime Minister Winston Churchill that a major Soviet counter-attack was planned, but withheld the details.

## Restarting oil production

With the Germans having captured Maikop, Technical Petroleum Brigade personnel were soon moving into the area, while the city became the headquarters for several formations, including 49th Mountain Corps, as well as two prisoner detention centres and a hospital. When the Germans reached Khadyzhensk (south-west of Maikop) in August 1942, they were horrified to see the complete destruction of the area's oil drilling facilities. On 8 September 1942, a month after the German troops captured Maikop oil fields, Dr Günther Schlicht of Tactical Petroleum Brigade reported progress, but also that partisan activity from groups such as the 'People's Avengers' and

A 3rd Technical Mineralöl Brigade worker salvages what he can from the largely destroyed facility. (NARA)

others had resulted in oil worker deaths and equipment damaged or destroyed. To assist the German position, Red Army deserters and nationalists were active in combating Communist guerrillas and Soviet forces.

According to a German report, the destruction of Maikop's oil derricks and related facilities would take years to completely repair, as everything that could be blown up had been destroyed or damaged, and bore holes had had concrete and iron dumped into them. With road transport capacity rudimentary and rail lines destroyed, transporting heavy equipment was nearly impossible. As an indication of how far removed from the front line – and reality – high-ranking Party officials were, following the capture of the oil facilities south of Maikop, Göring inquired when German forces could begin fuelling their vehicles directly from the region. On being presented an accurate assessment of the situation, specifically that the wells had been clogged with debris, he demanded to know why they could not just 'drill them out with something like a giant corkscrew?'

3rd Technical Mineralöl Brigade surveying for the construction of one of the unit's ten portable distillation installations in Neftegorsk on 16 October 1942. Such facilities were used to separate kerosene, gasoline, and diesel elements before they were processed further. (NARA)

# ANALYSIS

## The military objectives

Although Fölkersam's 'Wild Bunch' had conducted a daring mission in which they infiltrated deep into the Soviet rear and remained undetected in the Maikop area for a week, they only completed one of their two objectives. Prior to the arrival of friendly conventional forces, they weakened the city's defences and sowed confusion, which aided Wiking and 13th Panzer Division when they arrived on 9 August en route for Tuapse and the Black Sea coast. Had the Germans been operationally able to cut off and eliminate the retreating Red Army from crossing the Don River, and later getting to the Western Caucasus foothills, Soviet resistance along the various passes would have been greatly reduced. Unable to prevent the destruction of most of the region's oil facilities, even had the Brandenburgers been completely successful, the Germans had no viable plan to transport what crude oil they expected to capture or refine, either locally or to the west.

Since Operation *Blau*'s commencement on 28 June 1942, Soviet resistance in the south had been intermittingly stiff, but otherwise plagued by confusion, retreats, and desertion. The rapid German battlefield tempo largely prohibited the Soviets from regaining their operational balance, and although the German prisoner hauls were low compared to *Barbarossa* the year before, to Hitler it indicated an eventual Red Army collapse in the sector in 1942. Closer inspection, however, showed an attacker that was as resource-strapped as the defender, with neither side able to effectively recoup losses in men and materiel incurred over the last year. For the Germans, it meant having to prioritize and reallocate available assets at the expense of other formations. The winter of 1941–42 rarely permitted German units to withdraw from the combat zone to conduct a regular training programme in preparation for the summer campaign. However successful Manstein's victory in the Crimean Peninsula had been, in mid-May 1942, German commanders redirected many of these air assets to the Kharkov sector to help defeat Timoshenko's initial offensive aimed at destroying Heeresgruppe Mitte. Combined with the German casualties incurred in reducing the Crimean port of Sevastopol, *Blau* suffered delays, and prompted senior commanders to adopt a complicated, phased campaign, with each stage requiring successful completion of its sequential goals.

As the plans for the German 1942 summer offensive required the enemy to largely adhere to the flawed or failed tactics from the previous year, the Soviets' deviation progressively hampered progress, interrupted timetables, and used up valuable men and materiel. Unable to operationally halt the enemy, who retreated ever deeper into the interior, the Germans lacked the fuel and functioning transportation assets to capitalize on the situation. As in 1941, Hitler, and many senior German commanders continued to underestimate Soviet strength and resolve, a mindset that was reinforced in large measure by the after-effects of Stalin's purges in the late 1930s, including generally poor leadership at every echelon and tactics that were commonly unsophisticated. Persistence had increasingly turned what had been anticipated to be a short campaign into a global war of attrition, and much as had happened in 1941, the Germans had defeated their adversary, but failed to annihilate it.

Considering that the distance from Rostov-on-Don to Baku (1,117km) was just shy of the distance that First Panzer Army had travelled to get to Rostov-on-Don since the start of *Barbarossa*, *Edelweiss* could only have succeeded if German forces, especially armour, mechanized, and motorized, were up to strength, in sufficient numbers, and adequately supported to maintain their battlefield potency and endurance. As the campaign was increasingly subordinated to the fight for Stalingrad, fewer men and materiel were available to cover an ever-greater area in the Caucasus. In July 1942, for example, some of the divisions from Heeresgruppe Mitte had frontages as great as 60km, six times the doctrinally stated distance on the defensive. It is worth noting that by this time the Germans were holding over 7,500km of frontage in Western Europe, excluding Finland, North Africa, and the Balkans, and to compensate, they relied on ill-equipped and poorly led Italian, Hungarian, and Rumanian allies.

## The oil question

Throughout *Blau*, and especially in the Caucasus, the Germans struggled with a number of issues that kept them from securing the latter and achieving their ultimate goal of capturing Grozny or Baku. What oil facilities they overran south-west of Maikop proved a disappointment, and the TBM teams only began extraction in December, which during the following month

Workers of the 3rd Technical Mineralöl Brigade construct an enclosure on 16 October 1942 for this trio of locomotive-style firebox boilers. A fire in the structure's rear produced hot gases that passed through several flutes (fire tubes) to the smoke box and funnel. The surrounding cylinder contained water that was correspondingly converted into steam, transferred along a pipe, and used to provide drilling power to the derrick. (NARA)

A pair of 3rd Technical Mineralöl Brigade members attempts to control a section of drill pipe at Neftegorsk on 16 October 1942. By the time German forces had secured such facilities, the retreating Soviets had clogged the wells with stones, bricks, and concrete, making most inoperable. (NARA)

amounted to just 13 wells producing a paltry 70 barrels per day. Projections of 2,000 barrels per day were made for the following April, and as much as 26,000 barrels per day by the end of 1943, but these were never realized and fell far short of their 52,000 barrels per day (19 million barrels each year) during peacetime. Given that German pre-war annual consumption totalled 44 million barrels, and consumption greatly increased during the war, Maikop's exploitation would have been of relatively minor value even if functioning at capacity. Instead, the retreating Soviets dismantled or destroyed the area's oil producing facilities, which often included pouring concrete, debris, and saltwater into the wells, rendering them permanently useless.

A third worker assists with a makeshift branch, while additional drill pipe sections lies nearby. Once these sections were installed, a pumpjack assembly would be used to pump the oil to the surface when underground pressure was insufficient. (NARA)

In any case, during the original planning to secure the Caucasus oilfields – as part of Operation *Barbarossa* – Hitler had largely avoided any meaningful discussion of a seemingly critical question that had vexed Ludendorff a quarter-century earlier: how to transport captured oil back to Reich refineries. In March 1941, one month after Albert Speer took over command of the Reich Ministry for Armaments and Munitions, the ministry provided OKW, which directed Germany's war effort (minus the Eastern Front under OKH) and controlled Army, Navy, and Luftwaffe finances, with a detailed report stating that even if the Caucasus oilfields and facilities could be captured intact, at

most just 10,000 tons per month could be transported to Germany with presently available resources, and even if the Black Sea could be rendered safe for shipping, all available Danube River tankers were presently allocated to transporting Rumanian oil. An Oberkommando der Marine (OKM, Naval High Command) memorandum on 9 May 1941 added that eliminating the Soviet naval presence in the Black Sea to create safe, stable routes to Rumanian ports (and likewise that of the British in the Mediterranean to secure routes through the Dardanelles to Greek and Italian destinations) was a prerequisite to continuing the war. While this was unlikely in 1942, other options were debated including constructing makeshift concrete river boats, and transferring Vichy French and Italian ships eastward to assist. Ultimately, Hitler deferred a solution, believing the situation could be adequately addressed following the *Barbarossa* campaign's successful conclusion sometime in October 1941, after which the Germans would transition to winter positions.

A steam boiler on 16 October 1942 at Neftegorsk showing its top-mounted dome and regulator that controlled the amount of power-producing, superheated steam passing through the vertical section of pipe. A safety valve/lever is affixed to the front, while a pipe and flow control wheel inducted water. (NARA)

## The broader campaign

Based on the summer campaign's progress and apparent success, Hitler's views that the Red Army was on the verge of defeat prompted him to issue the key directive of the campaign on 23 July. Impatient at *Blau's* slow pace and anxious of the Allies establishing a 'Second Front' in Western Europe, he decided to speed things up by splitting the German attack, with Heeresgruppe A taking Rostov-on-Don and the Caucasus, and Heeresgruppe B advancing in almost the exact opposite direction for Stalingrad and the Volga River. Rather than a carefully considered offensive with a defined *Schwerpunkt* (focal point) and a decentralized chain of command designed to best enable commanders on the spot to make decisions and act with maximum effectiveness, Hitler, having steadily usurped control of the German military from the General Staff, promoted a rigid, amateurish, and centralized structure in which he micromanaged events from hundreds of kilometres away. Barely able to supply one advance at a time, the Germans had been strapped with two.

Compared to the Soviets, the Wehrmacht's much greater ratio of administrative and logistics personnel to those in combat roles, in part due to their generally superior albeit maintenance-intensive technologies, further minimized what reserves could be fielded. Hitler's insistence on creating additional Panzer divisions without a commensurate increase in assets such as armour, artillery, and transport (German manufacturing having expected a relatively short war and not having transitioned to wartime quotas) meant

A cylindrical oil storage tank near Neftegorsk, 16 October 1942. Its flat roof is likely a floating variety that rose and fell with the liquid's level, while the vertical feed line was used for its refilling. (NARA)

that the well-conceived formations were correspondingly imbalanced and forced to relinquish much of their strength to other units. The fact that until November 1942 up to 45 per cent of all trains transporting supplies for the Wehrmacht fighting in the Caucasus were blocked by partisan activities there only added to a host of operational handicaps, including limited fuel and a flawed plan, and further undermined the German effort, which was exacerbated the further they advanced into a still-defiant Soviet Union.

In World War II Germany had a theatre of operations, an occupied area, and the zone of the interior, with each needing a steady stream of manpower the longer the war continued. To distribute the insufficient forces over the three zones in such a way that the front was not shortened and the other two areas could perform their diverse tasks was almost an unsolvable problem. At *Barbarossa's* start, the ratio of non-combatants to combat personnel was 3:10. Three months later it changed to 6:10, and by October 1942 it was roughly even numbers of each, an imbalance that only increased during the war due to the latter suffering disproportionate casualties. To compensate, administrative and logistic personnel were increasingly used to replace battlefield losses, but they did not eliminate the underlying problem that each branch of the German armed forces, the Labour Organization, Organization Todt, and other groups each maintained their own logistics and services systems that lacked consolidation and increased the disproportion of the figures.

In contrast, the more primitive, simple Soviet system averaged one non-combatant to ten fighters. To replace combat losses, the Red Army simply drew replacements from the supply and rear services or the civilian population, something outside the Western military mindset. The Luftwaffe ratio of aircraft crews to non-combatants was particularly unfavourable, as evidenced in 1942; in the still-peaceful west, 300 signal communication personnel supported each combat-ready aircraft. To acquiesce to army demands for additional personnel, Göring provided more than 150,000 men, which instead of replenishing existing formations were used to create new Luftwaffe field divisions, which in turn added yet another organization and supply system. Manpower was needed to secure and maintain the lines of communication between the front and the homeland, administration, control, and security of the occupied areas, the mobilization and supervision of agriculture and industry, and to counter the growing partisan problem. The great space and very foreign environment also had a detrimental psychological effect on the German troops that was accentuated the longer they remained in the field.

By late August, Hitler had grown increasingly frustrated by the lack of progress in capturing the Caucasus, even though it was a situation for which he was responsible. By remaining unrealistically optimistic that at least some oil facilities could be captured intact and begin producing for Germany in a relatively short period, he frittered away an excellent opportunity to act decisively. During August and early September 1942 the Luftwaffe possessed the means to inflict heavy damage on Baku, where some 80 per cent of Soviet oil was produced, at a time when the Red Air Force remained weak and largely ineffectual, in large part as many such assets had been allocated to defend other sectors, especially Moscow. Throughout the late summer and fall of 1942, Hitler's fixation on capturing Stalingrad prompted him increasingly to allocate air assets to the city's destruction. It also blinded him to a broader perspective and enabled the Soviets to quietly gather forces in the sector, which eventually destabilized the southern front by year's end.

By October 1942, Hitler reluctantly admitted that ground forces would likely not reach the main oilfields before adverse weather conditions forced them to take up winter positions. Unwilling to allow such a valuable asset

A 4th Mountain Division repair workshop at Karatschajewsk on 18 September 1942 some 200km southeast of Maikop. The two nearest trucks (Skoda H 6ST6-Ts) were used by the Germans and their Rumanian allies. (NARA)

Members of the elite 1st Gebirgsjäger (Mountain) Division look out over the Caucasus Mountains on 14 November 1942, with the range's highest point, Mt Elbrus, in the distance on the right. Six days after the formation reached the Klukhov Pass on 15 August, a small party from it and 4th Mountain Division ascended the higher of its two peaks (5,642m) as a show of skill and planted their respective unit and Reich war flags. (NARA)

to continue producing for the enemy, he decided the Luftwaffe could simply bomb them and inflict a severe blow, from which it would have taken at least several months to recover, and at a time when Allied oil supplies via the Arctic Sea would not immediately compensate. By October, however, the Luftwaffe's eastern bomber fleet was much reduced and many forward airfields had been badly damaged from enemy aerial attacks. With these assets allocated to Heeresgruppen A and B having been dispersed and depleted over the last several weeks, they would be unable to undertake Hitler's belated orders for 'massive attacks' on Baku's oilfields on 22 October. Had the Germans captured or destroyed these assets around Baku and Grozny, the Soviets would have been left with just 2.2 million tonnes of oil reserves and two oil refineries in Saratov and Ufa. Instead, they achieved neither goal and were soon ejected from the region as a result. Ironically, German efforts to capture the Caucasus oilfields did more to increase their fuel demand, in what was another example of the regime creating battlefield problems it was unable to solve.

# CONCLUSION

As Hitler had become increasingly fixated on capturing Stalin's namesake city, soon after the capture of Maikop Wehrmacht efforts in the Caucasus degraded to relatively static fighting for the various passes to the Black Sea. In an effort to secure these prized chokepoints, the Germans allocated specialist mountain formations, but with the Soviets having gained a respite, they were able to use the combat-modifying terrain to achieve relative parity in the rugged area. By late September 1942, Hitler began to doubt that Baku could be taken in 1942, and ordered air strikes on the oil storage tanks in Saratov, Kamysin and Aatrachan, and in mid-October on Grozny's refineries. In the further course of the German Caucasus campaign, which had concluded in mid-November, logistics had declined, but large quantities were saved by the repair of the Rostov–Mosdok railway. Had it not been for that supply artery, First Panzer Army's operations would have ended in an untenable position due to a lack of fuel.

With Germany's Italian, Rumanian, and Hungarian allies unable to protect the flanks at Stalingrad, on 19 November 1942 the Soviets initiated a major counter-attack that within four days had encircled the city, and Sixth Army and much of Fourth Panzer Army along with it. Unable to seal the breach in its front lines, German efforts in the southern theatre changed to the operational defensive, which soon forced the abandonment of what *Blau* had achieved. With Hitler unwilling to let the trapped formations break out to reach a Manstein-led relief effort, deeming their presence necessary to tie down enemy forces that would otherwise join the general Soviet push westward, the Red Army steadily recaptured the territory lost during the summer, and made for Rostov-on-Don and beyond. Threatened with being cut off, German and Rumanian forces in the Caucasus had to relinquish their hard-won gains. With hope of establishing a Reichskommissariat Kaukasus dashed, their anti-Soviet Chechen and Ingush tribal allies were left on their own to suffer NKVD retribution that included execution, imprisonment, or forced relocation.

**17 JANUARY 1943**

**Red Army begins operation that retakes Maikop**

The Soviet campaign to recapture the North Caucasus began on 17 January 1943, and the TBM was correspondingly ordered to evacuate with little notice. Not wanting the advancing enemy to make use of their efforts, they dismantled and removed what drilling and refining equipment they could, and destroyed some 10,000 tons of what had to be abandoned. Having withdrawn to its garrison base at Armavir, the advancing Red Army attacked the city one week later. With the Soviets having eliminated the Stalingrad pocket on 2 February 1943, additional forces could now be allocated to their general southern offensive. On 24 February, Göring decided that the TBM should cease operations in the Caucasus and transfer to Estonia to extract shale gas. Nevertheless, the Germans were able to extract about 4.7 million barrels from the Soviet Union, which ironically equalled the quantity that they would have received under the provisions of the friendship treaty of 1939 had they not invaded the country.

With the Wehrmacht having assumed an operationally defensive stance that would, with few exceptions, inexorably push to the Reich borders and beyond, Brandenburgers in the 'Wild East' were transferred west to conduct other operations, including anti-partisan missions in Yugoslavia (October), Küstenjäger motorboat patrols against the Soviet Navy (November), and joint Fallschirmjäger action in Tunisia (in the autumn). On 20 November, the organization was expanded to five regiments of three battalions each, as well as supporting battalions, but by February 1943, the formation's use as a special operations force was at an end. On 1 April 1943, it was renamed Brandenburg Division and assigned to conventional battlefield duties, although their staff remained in Berlin. In July, the Abwehr lost favour with Hitler after Canaris was implicated in the plot to kill him, and Sicherheitsdienst, the SS Security Service, took over many of its duties. Some 1,800 Brandenburgers were transferred to the Waffen-SS under Sturmbannführer Otto Skorzeny's commandos, where they continued to conduct the kinds of missions for which they were originally trained. Having received its final name change of the war, Brandenburg Panzergrenadier Division ended the conflict in Moravia. Post-war, many former members, like those from the Waffen-SS, enlisted in the French Foreign Legion and fought in French Indo-China where their skills proved an asset.

Having resisted the use of special operation forces for nearly three decades as part of a widespread effort to sever all traditions associated with Prussian militarism,

The 25mm 'For the Defence of the Caucasus' medal was awarded to Soviet military and civilian personnel who served in the region between July 1942 and 9 October 1943, and features two single- and one twin-engine aircraft flying above Mt Elbrus with three tanks moving across terrain covered by oil derricks. 'For our Soviet Motherland' is inscribed on the reverse. (PD) after the mismanagement of the 1972 Munich Olympics hostage situation Germany rekindled the concept. But instead of a military unit, as was the norm in other countries, the resulting Grenzschutzgruppe 9 der Bundespolizei (GSG 9) was made part of the police. In spite of political sentiment that was anathema to a resurgent German military, former unit commander Ulrich K. Wegener once stated that the GSG 9 embodied the same 'camaraderie and esprit de corps' as that within the Brandenburgers. Others, such as former Kommando Spezialkräfte (KSK) commander General Reinhard Günzel reiterated the hereditary link by stressing that his soldiers understood that their roots were with the Abwehr formation, and compared its unit badge with the Knight's Cross that symbolized their fathers' 'unprecedented achievements'.

# BIBLIOGRAPHY

## Primary sources

Bundesarchiv-Militärarchiv, Freiburg, Germany [BA/MA] RW 19/199: Wi Rue Amt Stab Z/SR, Nr. 1754/42 gKdos, Berlin, den 1. September 1942: Kriegswirtschaftlicher Lagebericht Nr. 36, August 1942.

BA/MA RW 19/202: Auszuege aus KTB, Wi Rue Amt/Stab (nur Mineraloel-betreffend), Beginn: 9.1.41. Vortrag Dr Schlicht (Mineraloel Brigade) beim Amtchef, 8.9.1942. Bericht über Maikop.

BA/MA RW 19/202: Wi Rue Amt Stab Z/SR, Die deutsche Treibstoffversorgung im Kriege. Abgeschlossen um die Jahreswende 1941/42.

BA/MA Wi Rue Amt/Ro, Technische Brigade Mineraloel. 5 June 1941–27 March 1942; 21 July–30 November 1942.

BA/MA Wi Rue Ant, Orientierung ueber die wehrwirtschaftliche Bedeutung der besetzten russischen Gebiete, Nr. 1-15.

BA/MA RW 19/202: Az 66 b 2134 WStb/W Ro III, Vortragsnotiz für Generalfeldmarschall Göring über Zielsetzung und Forderungen für die Weiterführung des Mineralöl-Bauprogramms, 31 Januar 1939, in Auszüge au KTB, Wi Rü Amt/Stab.

'The German Campaign in Russia: Planning and Operations (1940–1942)'. Dept of the Army Pamphlet No. 20-261a (Washington, DC 1955).

MS P-148 Reinhardt, Hellmuth, 'Mountain Warfare: A Brief Treatise Based on Operations of 1st Mountain Division in the Caucasus, Aug.–Sep. 1942', 1953.

MS D-154 Moelhoff, Klaus, 'Experiences with Russian Methods of Warfare and Their Utilization in Training at the Waffen-SS Panzer Grenadier School', 1947.

MS D-248 Steiner, Felix, 'Tactics of Mobile Units. Operations of the 5th Panzergrenadier Division "Wiking" at Rostov and the Maikop Oilfields (Summer 1942)', 1947.

MS D-254 Schulz, Paul, 'Combat in the Caucasus Woods and Mountains During Autumn 1942', 1947.

USAFHRA K113.106-153 Vol. 14: Der Inspekteur des Luftschutzes, Az. 41 Nr. 2099/42, g., den 21.8.1942, Betr.: Meldung der Luftflotte 4 vom 19.8.1942. 'Schaeden auf den Oelfeldern von Maikop and Krasnodar'.

USAFHRA 512.607: 'German Plans for Russian Oil', AMWIS No. 134, March 1942.

Memories Filipenko Ivan Romanovich – member of the Society of Maikop Garrison Officers.

Collection of memories of veterans of the 18th Army combat units in Tuapse, Taman, Novorossiysk and the Crimea.

## Secondary sources (books)

Buchheit, Gert, *Der Deutsche Geheimdienst: Geschichte der Militarischen Abwehr*, List Verlag (Munich, 1966).

Eichholtz, Dietrich, *Krieg um Öl: Ein Erdölimperium als deutsches Kriegsziel 1938–1943*, Leipziger Universitätsvlg (Leipzig, 2006).

Grechko, Andrei, *The Battle for the Caucasus*, University Press of the Pacific (Honolulu, HI, 2001).

Heinz, Friedrich Wilhelm, 'Von Wilhelm Canaris zur NKWD', manuscript (1949).

Kurowski, Franz, *The Brandenburger Commandos: Germany's Elite Warrior Spies in World War II*, Stackpole Books (Mechanicsburg, PA, 2005).

Kurowski, Franz, *The Brandenburgers: Global Mission*, Fedorowicz (Winnipeg, 1997).

Lefevre, Eric, *Brandenburg Division: Commandos of the Reich* (Special Operations Series), Historie and Collections (Paris, 2001).

Lucas, James, *Kommando – German Special Forces of World War Two*, Cassell (London, 1999).

Mende, Gerhard von, *Das Unternehmen*, Hase & Koehler (Mainz, 1986).

Schramm, P. E., (ed.), *Kriegstagebuch des Oberkommandos der Wehrmacht (Wehrmachtfuehrungsstab) 1940-1945*, Bernard & Graefe (Frankfurt am Main, 1961).

Skorzeny, Otto, *Meine Kommndounternehmen: Krieg ohne Fronten*, Limes-Verlag (Munich, 1976).

Spaeter, Helmuth, *Brandenburger: eine deutsche Kommandotruppe*, Dissberger (Düsseldorf, 1992).

Tielke, Wilhelm, *The Caucasus and the Oil: The German–Soviet War in the Caucasus 1942/43*, Fedorowicz (Winnipeg, 1995).

# INDEX

References to illustrations and plates are shown in **bold**. Captions to plates are shown in brackets.